"I personally felt touched, encouraged ... be an overcomer by faith and not a fai¹ ... iring read!"

—Rhianne Co. ... nce

"Anxiety in a man's heart wei, ... but an encouraging word makes it glad" (Proverbs 12:25, Amplified Version). As those who live according to the Spirit and not the five senses of our flesh, we are encouraged by Akeem's Word-based solutions to the age-old challenge of fear. Whatever our circumstances, he directs us without compromise or wavering to Jesus, the author and finisher of our faith and the sole source of true freedom, peace, and joy."

—Steve & Stephanie Edmonds, Cell Group Pastors

"This book, *The Fear Factor*, is like a train charging through the darkness of this world, bringing the light of truth, hope, and peace, including the opportunity of salvation. A truly gripping read!"

—Reverend Nigel Armstrong

"This is by far the most comprehensive book I have read on dealing with fear. It is relevant to business and personal life, teachers and counselors, Christians and non-Christians—to people from all walks of life."

—L.E. Gunn (Kent), Professional Editor

"*The Fear Factor* is a book of life to be embraced and cherished. It is useful for personal, professional, and spiritual development. It is the type of book you want to occupy a prominent position in your library, the type you want to recommend to your book clubs and local libraries."

—Kayode, *The Faith Factor* (UK)

"Having being involved with books for about two decades as an avid reader, reviewer, editor, author, bookstore proprietor, and organizer of Mid-Western Christian Book Fair, I know a good book when I see one. Here is a good book."

—Reverend Paschal, Mid-Western Book Fair

THE FEAR FACTOR

How to Recognize and Overcome Your Fear

Akeem Shomade

Bridge-Logos

Alachua, Florida

Bridge-Logos
Alachua, FL 32615USA

The Fear Factor
by Akeem Shomade

Printed in the United States of America.

Library of Congress Catalog Card Number: 2008927774
International Standard Book Number 978-0-88270-501-9

Unless otherwise indicated, all Scripture quotations are from the *Holy Bible: New International Version*, (NIV). Copyright ©1973, 1978, 1984 by International Bible Society. Used by permission of Zondervan Publishing House.

Scripture quotations marked KJV are from the *King James Version* of the Bible. Those marked NKJV are from the *New King James Version*. Those marked NASV are from the New American Standard Version. Others as indicated.

G218.316.N.m806.35250

DEDICATION

To my wife,
Rufiat Folahan Shomade
and
"The Boys"
Kazeem & Abiodun Shomade,
for your love, patience and support.

&

To my late mother, Seliat Amori
who personified love in action to her children
and her community at large.
I first learned about the love of God through you.
We are missing you—"Rest in Peace."

&

To my earthly father,
Bashiru Adio Shomade
For your care, love, and prayers.

TABLE OF CONTENTS

PREFACE ix

FOREWORD xiii

INTRODUCTION xvii

ONE: WHAT IS FEAR? 1

TWO: FEAR CHECKLIST 7

THREE: CAUSES OF FEAR 13

FOUR: FEAR OF FAILURE 27

FIVE: FEAR OF DEATH 51

SIX: FEAR OF CHANGE 75

SEVEN: FROM FEAR TO LOVE 103

EIGHT: FEAR OF MAN 133

NINE: FEAR OF THE LORD 157

TEN: THE VERDICT 183

APPENDIXES

Appendix 1: The Decision—Salvation Prayer Template 201

Appendix 2: Fear Checklist Notebook (Self-Help Section) 205

Appendix 3: Personal Daily Confession and Declaration 209

ACKNOWLEDGMENTS 211

PREFACE

This book is written from the heart of a counselor. Its intended readership is Christians struggling with issues of fear and anyone whose ministry is to help other people. I believe that covers the majority of us because we all have feared something or someone at a particular time or place in our lives, and as Christians we are called to be our brother's keeper.

However, this book also creates opportunities for unbelievers to learn about the wisdom of God or start a relationship with the Maker of Heaven and earth and in the process of discovering God receive deliverance from unhealthy fear.

In this book you will find elements of teaching, counseling, exhortation, exaltation, practical advice, personal testimonies, and encouragement. The main motive is to reveal the heart of the Father, who wants us, above all things, to allow perfect love to cast out our fears.

Our mind is like a battleground. It is full of bad thinking and has been contaminated by the world's perspective rather than having been nourished by the knowledge of God's will for us. If we give the enemy a foothold and he gains access to our minds, there is no telling the amount of havoc he can wreak.

Fortunately, the Spirit of God is not limited in any way by the magnitude of our fears. Thank God that nothing (except "self") can disqualify us from God's plan as we cooperate with His Spirit. We should not allow fear to crowd out faith in the visionary Father who designed, arranged, and spoke the whole universe into existence.

The Scriptures declare, "The fear of the LORD is the beginning of wisdom" (Psalm 111:10). It means that the only fear we are allowed to entertain is the healthy fear of God. We are talking about an awesome respect growing out of the greatness and power of our heavenly Father, the Creator. He is the one who sent His beloved Son to visit planet earth and set us free from every stronghold.

A stronghold is a fortified place where a power has some level of control. It is also used to describe a Christian with an inner condition where Satan still has power to control. Paul taught us in 2 Corinthians 10:4-5: "For the weapons of our warfare are not carnal but mighty in God for pulling down strongholds, casting down arguments and every high thing that exalts itself against the knowledge of God, bringing every thought into captivity to the obedience of Christ" (NKJV).

A stronghold involves having constant negative thoughts and doing things with the sole purpose of making a name for ourselves rather than to lift up Jesus. He (Satan) fills our minds with fear, scepticism, and doubt if we permit him to do so. Strongholds often include lust, pride, bitterness, unforgiveness, grudges, jealousy, envy, and fear. They can exist in the body and soul of a believer, but the spirit is sealed by the Holy Spirit who dwells in us (Romans 8:11). Christ wants to set us free from the enemy's strongholds: We do not have to be crippled by them anymore.

This book will focus on different aspects of fear, with the main emphasis on unhealthy fear. That is the unnatural and harmful emotion that has no basis of truth but that has an object. By an object, I refer to the existence of a person or thing to which an action or feeling is directed; and the presence of such an object is so real that it is perceived that such a thing or person is capable of causing us harm. It is not conducive to our health and is induced mainly by negative forces. It is irrational and a thief to our well-being as it paralyzes us from taking responsible actions in order to achieve our goals. In the context of this book, I may use fear and anxiety interchangeably.

Anxiety is a state of the mind whereby a person suffers from an abnormal apprehension, worry, and fear and is often accompanied by physiological signs. The states of anxiety and fear are sometimes inseparable. However anxiety is different from fear because it is devoid of an object and lacks a specific cause. A state of anxiety exists when concern is shown before a specific event. Fear, however, occurs at the point of a frightful event. One can be anxious about a forthcoming interview or examination or about speaking in the presence of a big crowd. The common factor is that most of our fears and anxieties never occur. They are sometimes birthed out of undue concern for our health, safety, financial stability, or ability to perform a given task.

In one of the *Star Wars* episodes, it is said, "Fear leads to anger; anger leads to hate; and hate leads to suffering." While I am not glorifying *Star Wars*, and such a comment may not be true in all cases of fear, I believe that unhealthy fear can lead to unnecessary suffering. We need to guard our minds against unhealthy fear.

It is my personal desire that every reader of this book will meet and embrace Jesus as the only one with the power to deliver us from all fears.

Are you curious enough? Do you seek the wisdom that comes from the divine Architect? I challenge you to read on. You will receive deliverance from the stronghold of unhealthy fear and give God the glory.

—Akeem Shomade
London, United Kingdom

FOREWORD

It stretches across the aquamarine horizon, a shimmering white rainbow; claiming the canopy characteristic of its seven-colored ephemeral mentor, which promises a pot of gold to those who can trace either its antecedents to the one side or its terminus to the other. But, unlike the evanescent rainbow, the new Wembley Stadium is solid concrete and metal and is being constructed with permanence in mind.

As I write this, I am sitting a few meters from this magnificent colossus in the only old building that is still standing in the regeneration project that has seen almost every other neighboring building demolished.

A gentle swing to and fro, at first in the idiom of a pendulum clock with measured regularity. Then a sense of urgency sets in as the ball and chain dangle from the apogee of the demolition crane head with malicious intent and capricious urgency toward the imposing concrete facade of the building next to ours. And then BAM! The ball strikes at the epicenter of the building. The sound and impact send shock waves all across the neighborhood. Silence. Nothing. The facade is still standing, looking decidedly defiant and seeming to ask "Is that all you have got?"

In reply, the ball and chain recommence their macabre dance of death and administer another death knell to the same spot as before. This time, the concrete facade cracks, gazes at its superstructure in unbelief, attempts groggily to remain on its feet, totters left and right like a drunk in Central London after a whole night of binge-drinking, and finally gives in to the superior force of the construction engineer's vision. In only a few short moments, what once was a stronghold lies in ruins awaiting the excavators and dump trucks whose task is somewhat more mundane and routine but crucial if the new building is to be erected on the site.

Every passerby marvels, shakes the head, hisses, and wonders why the building was put up in the first place if it was only going to be thrown down so ignominiously and ignobly.

As I read Akeem Shomade's book, *The Fear Factor*, each chapter was like the demolition ball and chain dealing fatal body blows to the different varieties of fear that assail not just virtually everybody in the natural world but sadly also the preponderance of the inhabitants and heirs of God's Kingdom, the Church.

He illuminates our hearts to the fact that fear is neither only instinctive emotions aroused by impending or imminent danger, pain, or evil, nor indeed purely the "body's natural response system that alerts us to the presence of danger and directs our focus toward self-protection;" but that fear could be a spirit that plagues, torments, tortures, and holds people captive.

The Fear Factor is the practical illustration of Paul's admonition to the Corinthian Church: "For though we live in the world, we do not wage war as the world does. The weapons we fight with are not the weapons of the world. On the contrary, they have divine power to demolish strongholds" (2 Corinthians 10:3-4).

Akeem, like the professional demolition expert, knows that to bring a stronghold down you must understand its very foundation, its components, and its superstructure. Borrowing a leaf from the Apostle Paul, he recognizes that strongholds begin as thoughts; in other words, thoughts are the building blocks of what will eventually become a stronghold.

The Fear Factor teaches you how to get every thought of fear in its diverse ramifications to come under the authority of Christ, to surrender to His service, and to pay obeisance in acquiescent obedience to the Servant King. This is because thoughts uncontrolled will run riot and become imaginations and "high things" that exalt themselves against the knowledge of God. Imaginations are a series of thoughts that engage in confuting arguments. Moffat calls them theories and ramparts thrown up to resist the knowledge of God, while Knox calls them conceits of men and barriers of pride. J.B. Phillips in turn calls them deceptive fantasies. And, finally, the New English Bible calls them sophistries.

Whatever you call them, left unchecked they develop into strongholds that become infinitely more difficult to demolish. The bottom line is that, like the logic of the passersby, why build it if it is only going to be demolished?

Akeem Shomade draws from his background as a former Muslim, his professional background as an actuary and financial consultant, his intellectual background and acute mental perspicacity, and his deep compassion as a Christian and a family man to present a book that is not only well-researched but well-written.

The constant call to the unsaved person who is reading, the Salvation Prayer Template in the Appendices Section, the Fear Checklist Notebook (Self-Help Section), the Personal Daily Confession and Declaration, as well as the Scriptures at the end of each chapter raise the book to the level of indispensability and everyday application. I recommend it wholeheartedly.

O ye fearful, get ready for the ride of your life on the "Truth Train," which will culminate in "Freedomsville." Be blessed!

—Pastor Michael Omawumi Efueye
Senior Pastor
House On The Rock
The London Lighthouse

Introduction

I have entitled this book *The Fear Factor* because I recognize that we all fear something! And whatever we fear can rob us of God's best for our lives. Together, we will identify the fear factors in our lives and apply the appropriate medicine of God's Word to cast them out.

I do not profess to be an expert on this subject. In fact, while writing this book, my world was rocked and I feared for the financial survival of my household as I was ridden with debt. I also feared dying prematurely without leaving any inheritance to support my wife and children because of a painful lump that suddenly appeared on my left breast. False alarm! Either the enemy was playing tricks on me or the Lord has healed me. I believe it was the latter. I praise God because by His stripes I have been totally healed; the pain and the lump are no more. I even entertained some level of anxiety for the success of this book. I wondered if the contents of this book were capable of ministering life to our fearful world.

For purposes of comparison, I also will talk about healthy fear. This type of fear is like a vitamin tablet designed to boost our immune system and vaccinate us against the evil seed the enemy tries to sow inside us. I use the analogy of vitamin tablets because they are designed to supply our bodies with substances that are essential in our diet for particular body processes. In the same way, healthy fear is a natural human emotion, designed by God to protect us. For instance, a healthy fear of fire prevents us from running into a burning building. Likewise, a healthy fear of disease prevents us from drinking water from a sewer.

Despite my personal fears and anxiety, I have now reached a place where I am able to declare, like the psalmist, "Even though I walk through the valley of the shadow of death, I will fear no evil, for you are with me; your rod and your staff, they comfort me." (Psalm 23:4).

What am I saying? Simply, that just like those who are open to the flu virus, we can be vulnerable to the spirit of fear and its symptoms. However, when we struggle with unhealthy fear, our focus should be on God's promises and on His finished work on the Cross of Calvary. Geoff Shattock of Worknet commented that an old preacher asserted that there are 366 references to 'fear not' in the Authorized Version of the Bible. If this is so, it shows that God really knows us and is well aware of our unholy alliance with the spirit of fear. Prior to sending us on a tough task, He has a habit of encouraging us positively against fear—"Do not be afraid" (Genesis 15:1).

The spirit of fear has been in an unholy partnership with mankind since the beginning of creation. Fear began in the Garden of Eden (Genesis 3:8-10) and it led mankind to run and hide from God. After mankind had disobeyed God, the merciful Father still showed up for a time of worship: Adam's response to His inquiry was, "I heard you in the garden, and I was afraid because I was naked; so I hid" (Genesis 3:10).

Adam and Eve tried to cover up their sin instead of repenting. They had set an unhealthy precedent for mankind, and because of their misdeed people today still live in fear of exposure and punishment. Living with this type of fear is a form of imprisonment and is contrary to God's desire for us.

I started by saying that we all fear something. It could be a fear of danger or failure. Generally mankind has a fear of death, and as a result we are unwilling to discuss this topic until confronted with death itself or when we have reached old age. Parents generally fear for their children's safety; they do not want them to be exposed to dangers in their daily routine. As a result they may prevent their children from learning to swim or to drive because they are afraid their children might drown or suffer untimely death in a motor accident.

Some are anxious about the unknown. Many people suffer from excessive anxiety about the success of their businesses or their jobs, and for the success or otherwise of the calling of God on their lives. Believe it or not, some have anxieties about knowing God intimately. By this I mean the unhealthy fear of submitting to the counsel of God and surrendering their individuality to Him.

Anxiety describes a situation where a person has a normal or abnormal apprehension—a painful uneasiness of mind with worry, tension, and fear. It is often accompanied by physiological signs as lives are in constant suspense, which lingers long after the danger has subsided.

The fear of God is different to anxiety—it involves worshiping the Lord with deep respect and devotion. Psalm 111:10 declares, "Reverence for the LORD is the foundation of true wisdom. The rewards of wisdom come to all who obey him. Praise his name forever!" (The New Living Bible).

This assertion was supported by the words of that faithful man called Job, when he said, "The fear of the Lord—that is wisdom, and to shun evil is understanding" (Job 28:28).

Job had just caught a revelation that man could not teach him wisdom. It took trials and tribulations for him to see the light. He was asserting that we all need a healthy fear of the Lord, not because God is looking for opportunity to punish us for our wrongdoing, but so that we may revere and exalt Him as our God who has all power and might in His hand and as the Creator of all things (see Genesis 1:1). Once we get to have a healthy fear of the Lord, we have understanding and do away with the things that do not bring glory to Him. That is what Job 28:28 means by ". . . and to shun evil is understanding."

We have quickly established that knowledge, wisdom, and understanding are derived from a healthy fear of the Lord. Our Father is a loving God, and He seeks a personal relationship with every one of us. He loves us so much "that He gave His one and only Son, that whoever believes in him shall not perish but have eternal life" (John 3:16).

If the fear of God is the beginning of wisdom, why are we anxious about knowing God intimately? The answer is rooted in our strange misconceptions of God. When we read about how God destroyed Sodom and Gomorrah (Genesis 19), we are afraid. We think it may be better not to know this God than to know and be destroyed by Him because of our doubt, mistrust, or sin. Or we think that if we accept His calling for us we will lose everything we have worked for all our lives. Or He will expose us for what we are.

The fear of knowing God is a fear of experiencing Him, of not being able to define and control Him, and of relating with Him. In short, it is a fear of being open to the future and to the deepest impulses within us.

The fear of knowing God is tied in to the fear of change. Here, I'm talking about change in our religious system, worldview, ethical practices, and identity in order that we may reflect the Father's original purpose for our lives.

ONE

WHAT IS FEAR?

Definition 1. The *Longman Modern English Dictionary* describes fear as the instinctive emotion aroused by impending or seeming danger, pain, or evil.[1] Believe it or not, it also talks about awe and reverence in the fear of God.

Definition 2. Some people regard FEAR as: False
                                          Evidence
                                          Appearing
                                          Real

Definition 3. Others define fear as the body's natural response system to that which alerts us to the presence of danger and directs our focus toward self-protection.

Definition 4. I describe a fearful person as someone filled with an anxious mind, eyes weary with longing, and a despairing heart. It is a person who lives in constant suspense, filled with dread both night and day.

My definition comes from Deuteronomy 28:65-67: "Among those nations you will find no repose, no resting place for the sole of your foot. There the LORD will give you an anxious mind, eyes weary with longing, and a despairing heart. You will live in constant suspense, filled with dread both night and day, never sure of your life. In the morning you will say, 'If only it were evening!' and in the evening, 'If only it were morning!'—because of the terror that will fill your hearts and the sights that your eyes will see."

None of the above perfectly defines fear because some fears are induced by spiritual forces that originate from Satan (as with Definition 4). Others are the body's natural responses designed by our Maker to protect us from impending danger (Definitions 1 and 3).

Yet there is a higher call to fear (respect), worship, and obey God for who He is as our Creator who made us perfectly in His own image. This is the fear of the Lord.

Definition 2 challenges us to let our faith defy fear and continue to believe in the day of trouble, not letting what we see or feel define us. It is a challenge to use our faith positively to crowd out unhealthy fear and focus on the Scripture that says, "The righteous will live by faith" (Romans 1:17).

Tim Jackson, in his book *When Fear Seems Overwhelming*,[2] asserts that scientists have discovered some bodily cells called the "amygdala," which function as a control center for our fear's response. These cells activate almost every needed system within the body to deal with the danger at hand. He adds that, when the system misfires, medical intervention is needed to restore balance in the brain, and a failure to do so may lead to undue levels of fear, anxiety, panic, and depression. While I believe that God uses doctors to treat people, it is important that we guard against thinking that fear or any other emotional response is simply a function of science. God has the final say on everything that concerns those who believe in Him.

Definition 3 fails to recognize that everything we are or have belongs to God (our abilities, talents, and such) and is therefore not our own. So we have nothing to lose and as a result nothing to fear. The problem is that we think things belong to us.

In addition, Definition 4 seems like fear that comes from a spiritual force induced by Satan. However, I must quickly point out that not all fear is a spirit; and that not all unpleasant emotions are wrong. We know that "God hath not given us the spirit of fear; but of power, and of love, and of a sound mind" (2 Timothy 1:7, KJV).

We also know that our Lord is a good God and that He works with our faith. The Bible says, "Without faith it is impossible to please God" (Hebrews 11:6).

Fear (like the devil) roars because it pretends to be like a lion; but when you confront it, it runs away! Jesus is the Lion of Judah.

Faith—The Opposite of Fear

How then do we build our faith in God? We do so by seeking Him diligently and believing His Word, for it is written, "The righteous will live by faith" (Romans 1:17).

We also know that "faith comes from hearing the message, and the message is heard through the word of Christ" (Romans 10:17).

The author of the Letter to the Hebrews defines faith as "being sure of what we hope for and certain of what we do not see" (Hebrews 11:1) and then goes on to list the great deeds that the people of Israel had accomplished "by faith" (2-40).

In the Synoptic Gospels, faith is the operative factor in many of Jesus' miracles. Jesus is impressed by the faith of the centurion and so heals his son (Matthew 8:5-13). Jesus marvels at the faith of those who brought the paralytic man (Matthew 9:2). When Jesus tells the father of a demon-possessed boy, "Everything is possible for him who believes [has faith]," the man responds, "I do believe; help me overcome my unbelief!" (Mark 9:23-24).

John's Gospel emphasizes having faith throughout and states its purpose as being to lead people to believe that Jesus is the Messiah, the Son of God (John 20:31).

God is the source of faith, and every good and perfect gift is from above, coming down from the Father of lights, who does not change like shifting shadows (James 1:17). He would not bless us today with a gift of faith and take it back tomorrow, only to replace it with fear.

Faith in God will give us inner peace when all we see around us is turmoil. The Scriptures tell us that faith is the gift of God (Ephesians 2:8). However, to get the best out of every gift, we need to use it. Likewise, we need to act out what we believe and obey His commands.

Did I hear you say, "For it is by grace you have been saved" (Ephesians 2:8) and therefore no human effort can contribute to our salvation? This statement is not only true, but it is also profound and delivers us from dead works.

May I declare boldly that our world is full of people to whom God has been speaking for a while—calling them, loving them—and yet they have resolved to harden their hearts or have allowed past experiences to cloud their judgment. All of us who fall into this category need to realize that no response to the love of God means no action—which means the loss of an opportunity to be restored into a loving relationship with God.

What has that to do with fear? Well, some of us are anxious of the unknown and as a result we walk by sight. We operate by the worldly principle that "seeing is believing". When the disciples of Jesus were facing the storm on the sea, they were very afraid. However, Jesus responded by saying, "Why are you fearful, O you of little faith?" (Matthew 8:26, NKJV). Like the disciples, Jesus wants us to believe that our boat will not sink if He is in it with us.

Susan Jeffers, the writer of the famous book *Feel the Fear But Do It Anyway,* classifies fear into three levels:

Level A: Situation Oriented;

Level B: Ego Related; and

Level C: I can't handle it!

I have used some of Susan Jeffers' classifications below because I think we can all relate to them, and it is an established fact that simple and uncomplicated things are usually very effective. However, I need to mention that the levels described below are not in any particular order.

WHAT DO YOU FEAR?—THREE LEVELS OF FEAR[3]

Level A Fears—Situation Oriented

Almost certain to occur:

Getting old

Retirement

Children leaving familiar environment

Dying

Possible actions in the face of change:
> Decision making
> Career change
> Making friends
> Beginning or ending a relationship
> Asserting oneself
> Learning to drive
> Losing weight
> Public speaking (to gain/regain confidence).

You are not alone if you identify with some or all of the above.

Level B Fears—What If?
> What if I am rejected?
> What if I meet with people's disapproval?
> What if I fail?
> What if I lose my image in the eyes of others?

This deals with the inner states of mind rather than with exterior situations. This reflects our sense of self and abilities to handle this world. Fear of rejection will affect every area of our lives—friends, intimate relationships, job interviews, and such.

Level C Fears—The "I can't" Syndrome
I can't handle illness. I can't handle making a mistake. I can't handle getting old. I can't handle losing my job or not getting the job. I can't handle being alone. I can't handle making a fool of myself.

Some of us may say, "I fear nothing or no one". My honest reply to that person is, "Well done, my Brave Heart." But can you really say, "I've never had a true encounter with fear in my life?" If your answer is still "Yes," please permit me to awaken your senses and remind you that you may have lost touch with the past or that the truth is not in you.

You may quote to me: "For God hath not given us the spirit of fear; but of power, and of love, and of a sound mind" (2 Timothy 1:7, KJV).

Well done! You are well versed in Scripture. But I'm sure the Holy Spirit will remind you about the time when you feared for safety of your child, spouse, friends, or loved ones!

In 1 Timothy 4:12, the Apostle Paul had to build up Timothy's confidence by encouraging him to be focused, not allowing anyone to intimidate him. Apparently, lack of confidence and experience and the fear of intimidation had prevented Timothy from being effective at the initial stages of his ministry. Paul became an effective instrument in removing the gremlin of fear from Timothy by using the technique of love.

We all fear something, and the Lord is well aware of our concerns. It is not a bad thing for us to feel the full fragility of our lives, providing it makes us turn to the Giver of light. We ought to remember that the Spirit of God gives us the power to face our foes and imparts in us the love to overcome evil with good and the discipline to persevere through our trials. In fact, God is greater than the most severe threats we could ever face in life. In Him we have the power to turn fear into faith.

End Notes

1. *Longman Modern English Dictionary*. Longman, 1976.
2. Jackson, Tim. *When Fear Seems Overwhelming*.
3. Jeffers, Susan. *Feel The Fear And Do it Anyway*, "Three Levels of Fear" (Pages 13-15). Arrow Books, 1991.

TWO

Fear Checklist

We can now take a second look at Level A Fear as mentioned above. Please be honest with yourself when identifying which category of fear you subscribe to and asking yourself why that is. List your reasons in the notebook provided at the end of this book (Appendix 2), and find the solution to your identified fears in the Word of God. It is possible that the solution to your fears may have been discussed in an earlier passage, or you may find the solution as you continue to read this book.

Level A Fears

As for me when writing the manuscript of this book, I completed the Fear Checklist and found that in Level A Fears, I subscribed to the fear of dying. Yes, I know that physical death is the door to eternal life for those who believe in Jesus Christ. Those who believe are promised a glorious future—the resurrection of the body and everlasting life (John 11:25).

However, I realized I would not like to die right then because I had yet to complete my earthly assignment. I must finish the work just as Jesus did, as He empowers me to do so. Then I suddenly realized that no pain, disease, or cancer would rob me of the joy of completing the work that the Father has sent me. Jesus took all my infirmities, died in my place, and by His stripes I am healed (Isaiah 53:5).

I would be lying, though, if I said that I had not been afraid. For a moment I thought about all God's promises and assignments for me. I thought of my wife and children and of the current provision for my household. In fact, it reminded me of the famous prophet who died leaving nothing but debt to the extent that his children were almost sold into a life of slavery. Praise God for divine intervention![1] But then I remembered the beautiful end to that story: God's bountiful provision above and beyond what they could ever have imagined. My God is faithful. He watches over His Word and looks for every opportunity to bring it to pass. Suddenly the Word of God came to light, that: "I was young and now I am old, yet I have never seen the righteous forsaken or their children begging bread." (Psalm 37:25).

Let us be reminded that Jesus' disciples were initially afraid when they saw Him walking on the sea. They thought it was a spirit, and they cried out with fear. Jesus had to calm their fears by revealing himself to them: "It is I; be not afraid" (Mark 6:50, KJV).

Jesus is saying the same to us about fear. Like the disciples of old, He is in our boat; and we do not need to entertain fear, as it paralyzes us.

LEVEL B FEARS

This deals with the inner state of our mind rather than any exterior situation. These fears reflect our sense of self and our ability to handle whatever this world throws at us. Fear of rejection will affect every area of our lives—friendship, intimate relationships, job interviews—and also works against our personal progress. This fear may even prevent us from reaching the Lord's purpose for our lives. Do not fear, as God is able to turn failure into success. He can use closed doors to redirect our energy into what really matters and also lead us to the summit of excellence.

Academic/Business Failure

For those of us who have failed an examination or in business, it seems as if our world has crashed, and we have lost everything. We need to be assured that the power that resurrected Jesus is still available to us and that at the appointed time and season, we will laugh again. Like Job, all that we have lost will be restored as a double portion, so exchange your fear for faith! The author of Hebrews defines faith as:

"The assurance of things hoped for, the conviction of things not seen" (Hebrews 11:1, NASV).

Fear of Rejection

When everyone has rejected us, we need to remember that Jesus was also rejected and humiliated by His people. After Jesus opened the eyes of the man born blind, using spittle and mud (John 9:6-7), the Jews were filled with jealousy. They decided that anyone who acknowledged that Jesus was the Christ would be excommunicated from the synagogue and from many social events (John 9:22). Have we not read in Scripture that: "The stone the builders rejected has become the capstone; the Lord has done this, and it is marvelous in our eyes" (Matthew 21:42).

That is our portion, too, in Jesus' name.

Joseph also was rejected by his brothers, thrown into an empty cistern, and later sold to a life of servitude. They figured, "We'll see what comes of his dreams" (Genesis 37:20). People of God; be prepared for the world's reaction to your vision, for the world will often misunderstand you. They stripped Joseph of his colorful coat because they were jealous and did not want him having any authority over them. Just as Joseph's brothers resented his authority, you can be sure that the devil will fight to strip you from recognizing or using your God-given authority. The good news is that Joseph held on to his dream in prison, practiced diligence, and quietly nurtured God's calling within himself no matter the circumstances. Proverbs 18:16 teaches: "A man's gift maketh room for him, and bringeth him before great men" (KJV).

Joseph's gift eventually took him to the palace where he interpreted the Pharaoh's dream and became the prime minister of Egypt in the process. Do not let rejection or circumstances shake you loose from your God-given dreams.

LEVEL C FEARS

This deals with poor self-image and overreliance on our own strength, as opposed to relying on God who created all things and is able to breathe new life into every situation.

If anyone is saying, "I cannot handle illness," I applaud your honesty. But the one who said in Exodus 15:26, "I am the LORD, who heals you," lives inside you. He allowed himself to be crushed for our iniquities and took the punishment that brought us peace upon himself. The Scripture declares that "by His wounds we are healed" (Isaiah 53:5). We need to believe His Word and enter into His finished work.

Fear of Being Alone

We need to remember that the great ever-present and all-knowing God is with us always until the end of time (Matthew 28:20).

Fear of Old Age

Is this your gremlin? Old age is the dawn of wisdom and the contemplation of the truths of God from the highest standpoint. The joys of old age are greater than those of youth as we mature in the ways of the Lord. We also need to recognize that living as old as Methuselah is not necessarily a sign of God's blessing. But if we honor our parents and obey and serve God with all our heart, His promise to us in return is old age. Failure to do God's will can attract disaster and sudden death (Job 36:11-12).

Conversely, dying young is not necessarily a curse. Jesus' life-span on this earth was short and effective. However, we must be encouraged not to delay in making a decision to follow Christ until tomorrow, as our lives are like a vapor that appears for a little time and then disappears (James 4:14).

Fear About Retirement and Old Peoples' Homes

Does this one cause you to tremble? When you have given yourself to worldly duties, please note that retirement provides a perfect opportunity to devote time to God's work and serve Him diligently. Serving God in capacities other than in our "worldly" jobs can be very rewarding. As we work in His vineyard, He will equip and empower us to do His will and to enjoy the kind of fulfilment that our previous work perhaps could not offer us. The truth is that we can do all things with Christ who strengthens us (Philippians 4:13). Once we know that we can handle anything that comes our way, what can we possibly have to fear? The true answer is nothing. However, we need to identify our gremlin, deal with it, and possess our possession.

END NOTES

1. 2 Kings 4:1-7, Story of the widow's oil.

THREE

Causes of Fear

In Levels A-C above, we have been exposed to various causes and degrees of fear. All I want to do in this chapter is to add more meat to the bones. Let us look at some of the causes of fear.

Ignorance

When we do not know what is already available to us, we tend to struggle needlessly. The prophet Hosea put it succinctly: "My people are destroyed from lack of knowledge" (Hosea 4:6).

In part, the ignorance stems from our utter disregard for God's Word, and in part from the failure of some ministers to teach the undiluted Word of God without favour or hypocrisy. Some ministers do not sufficiently promote God to His people as the true source of life. Instead they emphasize the sins of the people and relish their wickedness. They water down the gospel for financial purposes.

Such ministers have allowed the people to substitute them for the Lord. They have turned their blind eyes to the fraudsters, the adulterers, spiritual prostitutes (those who worshiped other gods in the week and suddenly become pious on Sunday). Their people have lived in a constant position of spiritual ignorance because of a shepherd's failure.

These people reason that if the shepherd has not spoken against their misdeeds, then their misdeeds must be all right with God. They think it is acceptable to consult palm readers, crystal ball readers, occultists, necromancers, and all forms of spirits that are not of God. They have forgotten that the great "I am" is a jealous God who commands that we worship no other gods beside Him (Exodus 20:4-5).

Spiritual prostitution is not acceptable to God. Money does not rival our God, nor does it give the peace that passes man's understanding because its sphere of influence is limited. Have you ever noticed that a rich person has many "friends" but as soon as the person hits hard times, their many "friends" suddenly disappear?

The "friends" might even become such a person's worst critics and accuse him or her of wasteful spending. On the other hand, remember God's promise to you: "I am with you always, to the very end of the age" (Matthew 28:20).

Jesus put it this way: "I have told you these things, so that in me you may have peace. In this world you will have trouble. But take heart! I have overcome the world (John 16:33).

This speaks of victory over unhealthy fears. In Him you have a peace that money, drugs, and illicit sex cannot buy. All these can offer you is more trouble, but rejoice—the all-knowing God has gone ahead of you to make all crooked paths straight. He says that, though the world gives you tribulation, He has overcome all the misery on your behalf.

Past Experience

At times, our experience prevents us from attaining God's best for our lives. Any time we want to move on, the enemy takes pleasure in reminding us about our past failures and gives us, or we give ourselves, thousands of reasons why we should not make that business move or why we should not try to restore our relationship with God. Simply, the enemy uses the spirit of fear to keep us stagnant.

The solution is an implicit faith in Jesus. Let the power of faith stifle out that fear. As we give our past experiences to Jesus, we will receive the faith to soar with eagles' wings and His love will cast out all fear. Scripture says, "Everything that does not come from faith is sin" (Romans 14:23).

If we doubt, we are not obeying God but rather believing the lies of the enemy. James 1:6-8 (NKJV) says, "But let him ask in faith, with no doubting, for he who doubts is like a wave of the sea driven and tossed by the wind. For let not that man suppose that he will receive anything from the Lord; he is a double-minded man, unstable in all his ways" (James 1:6-8, NKJV).

This tells me that, if we look to God for truth, guidance, and transformation into His likeness, He will in turn lighten our path and guide us into His plans for our lives. And as a result of the faith placed solely in Him, failure becomes a divorced friend to us for, "No eye has seen, no ear has heard, no mind has conceived what God has prepared for those who love him" (1 Corinthians 2:9).

Paul admonished us in Philippians 3:13-14 that we should forget what is behind and strive toward what is ahead. This is the new thing the Lord is doing in our lives, so that we can be all that He has purposed for us.

Pride

This is an attitude of the heart, and it is a cousin of fear as they are members of the same unholy family. It is a spirit of fear, disguised as pride, that when confronted with the Word of God gives birth to humility. Pride keeps us from accepting the love of Christ and from accepting that our nature is sinful. Instead of repenting of our sin, we continuously claim to be righteous, which becomes an obstacle to entering into the finished work of Christ. It breeds self-deception, which separates us from God (Proverbs 14:12).

Jesus said, "Unless you change and become like little children, you will never enter the kingdom of heaven" (Matthew 18:3).

I believe our Savior is stressing here the need for every Christian to strive for humility and the need to be receptive to the Spirit of God with an open mind, just like a little child. However, we must also be wise to the cunning nature of the enemy, as he disguises pride as humility. This occurs when we reject what God says about us and, through fear, lure ourselves into a false sense of humility instead of declaring that we are the righteousness of Christ.

At times, we are afraid of people's opinions of us, which prevent us from speaking out the words of the Father. He wants us to minister to our colleagues and neighbors; yet we refuse to speak about Him in our pride, partly because we are afraid of being classified as a freak or as different. The next time the Lord makes a demand of us to speak His words and we feel apprehensive, we need to remember the words of Jesus in Matthew 10:33: "Whoever disowns me before men, I will disown him before my Father in heaven."

Am I creating another fear by reminding you of the above Scripture? The answer is no. I am simply using it for emphasis to cement in your mind the need to fear the Lord above men.

Pride is one of the seven things the Lord hates, according to Proverbs 6:17-19. This is supported by Proverbs 8:13, where the Lord says, "I hate pride and arrogance." If the above is not enough to convince you, consider the result of pride according to Proverbs 11:2: "When pride comes, then comes disgrace, but with humility comes wisdom."

Are you convinced now that we have fulfilled the Scriptural requirement that says, "Every matter may be established by the testimony of two or three witnesses" (Matthew 18:16 & Deuteronomy 19:15)?

Paul puts it this way: "As for me, God forbid that I should boast about anything except the cross of our Lord Jesus Christ. Because of that cross, my interest in this world died long ago, and the world's interest in me is also long dead" (Galatians 6:14, New Living Bible).

Other results of pride are shown below.
- Pride brings contention (Proverbs 13:10).
- Pride brings destruction (Proverbs 16:18).
- A man's pride shall bring him low (Proverbs 29:23).
- Pride defiles the man (Mark 7:21-23).
- Pride brings condemnation as of the devil (1 Timothy 3:6).

As we can see from the above consequences of pride, we know that God's grace is upon the humble and that He opposes the proud (James 4:6, 1 Peter 5:5). This reinforces the assertion that humility is the solution to pride. Brethren, purpose in your heart to be free from the deceptive spirit of fear and its cousin pride.

CONCERN ABOUT THE FUTURE

Unhealthy concerns about our future survival and well-being may cause us to entertain anxiety and fear. The enemy then feeds on our state of mind by applying additional fuel to our minds; and, as we feed on his lies, we light the fire that leads to disaster. We begin to work on the basis that the situation is likely to get worse. Many opinion polls confirm that the majority of people regard the future with fear, which explains our high level of anxiety and collective insecurities.

Matthew 6:25-34 encourages us to substitute our worries with the assurance of God's provision. We must note that Matthew was not aloof to our earthly needs; rather he emphasizes that everything we require may be found in the Lord when we seek Him first above all other things.

We need to get hold of the present. Making the right decision today is vital—our actions today are directly proportionate to the result we get in the future. We need to align ourselves with the one who has the power to influence the future so that we may live the rest of our lives in prosperity.

DISPOSITION TO PANIC

When we panic, we inflate the problem. By doing so, we may overlook the possible solution. The news we hear on a daily basis may increase our disposition to panic as we worry about our savings and investments, the safety of our children, and of our jobs. We tend to lose all sense of direction when we are in a state of panic.

When the basic needs of life are not met, our insecurity leads to a dismantling of family ethics; parents let their child-rearing standards slip, and the diminished sense of control leads to wayward children wreaking havoc on society. The result is a social time bomb ticking and waiting to explode. We must learn to trust in God and in His provision.

Danger

One of the definitions of fear in the previous chapter describes it as the instinctive emotion aroused by impending or apparent danger, pain, or evil. We are in danger when faced with the possibility of being injured or killed or when faced with the likelihood that something unpleasant may happen. We tend to become fearful when the source of our security has been removed. Adam was the first to be faced with the realities of life. The probability of danger occurring to his family increased when he was evicted from Eden (Genesis 3:24). The safety mechanism provided by the angels inside the Garden had been removed. God sentenced Cain to a life of restless wandering on the earth for killing his brother Abel, and he immediately became fearful for his safety—"Whoever finds me will kill me" (Genesis 4:14).

Just as Paul suffered from real and imaginary fears (2 Corinthians 7:5), Cain also was exposed to external fear and became anxious for his safety. As Christians, we must remember that Jesus has overcome the world (John 16:33) and that we are secure in Him. It is this assurance that made the psalmist declare, "He who dwells in the shelter of the Most High will rest in the shadow of the Almighty. I will say of the LORD, 'He is my refuge and my fortress, my God, in whom I trust'" (Psalm 91:1-2).

Inadequate Sleep

Psalm 127:2 (KJV) tells us that "he giveth his beloved sleep." We must understand that to rest is not idleness, and to take time out is biblical and not a waste of time. There is time to work and time to play, time to cry and time to laugh. All these emotions are built into man. Human beings need a minimum of eight hours of sleep to be healthy and to function adequately. Sleep is essential in order to produce joy and vitality in life. In his book *The Power of Your Subconscious Mind,*[1] Joseph Murphy says that medical researchers have found sleep deprivation to precede psychotic breakdowns.

I have noticed that when I am really tired due to lack of sleep, a range of strange thoughts and emotions creep into my mind, and I can be unusually miserable and fearful of the future to the extent that

I forget the provisions of God. The mind plays tricks on us when we are very tired, and we become less tolerant, less loving, and have a very hard time thinking, feeling, and acting like Jesus.

David declares in Psalm 3:5, "I lie down and sleep; I wake again, because the LORD sustains me."

When we go to sleep, our Lord sustains us, and the things we worry about are actually safe in His loving hands. Surely, I am not alone in this sinful habit of not allowing myself enough sleep. Do you see yourself in this? If you relate to this, sleep may just be the answer! For others, please also add this simple gem to your defensive armor.

The Lord provided sustenance and rest for Elijah during his moment of discouragement. He sent an angel to provide food and drink for Elijah because our God knew the journey was too much for him. The Scriptures record in 1 Kings 19:1-9 that Elijah went to sleep at least three times (verses 5, 6, & 9). Without ignoring the power of God to sustain us, I believe that we should create time for sleep, food, and regular exercise, even if we are busy doing God's work. It replenishes our body and keeps us focused.

Jesus wants everyone to enjoy life abundantly, and part of that includes work, rest, and holiday time. He led by example because He himself took every opportunity to rest, be still with the Father, and meditate on His Word. God rested on the seventh day after working at Creation for six days.

Without encouraging laziness, I can safely say that it's all right to take time off and rest because lack of proper rest can make a person nervous and fearful just as Paul was in 2 Corinthians 7:5-7. In some cases this could be the answer to our prayers and a solution to our fears.

NEGATIVE SPIRITUAL FORCES

Definition 4, in the previous chapter, describes a fearful person as someone filled with an anxious mind, eyes weary with longing, and a despairing heart. A person who lives in constant suspense, filled with dread both night and day (Deuteronomy 28:65-67). It is most likely that negative spiritual forces are actively involved in the situation above with the sole purpose of intimidating and preventing people from excelling. From the beginning Satan prevented Adam and Eve from enjoying the provisions of God. He attempted to circumvent the higher calling of Jesus, but thank God that our Savior knew His purpose on earth. The Scriptures warned us to be alert and wise to Satan's intimidating tactic of prowling around like a roaring lion (1 Peter 5:8).

Satan would tempt people to sin and immediately accuse them. Sometimes he brings false accusations against God's people with the aim of discrediting us. A classic example is found in Job when God was praising Job for being a dedicated and righteous son. Satan replied, "Does Job fear God for nothing?" (Job 1:9).

Satan boldly accused the man that God had just commended and suggests that Job's righteousness was self-serving and dependent solely on what God could do for him.

In Zechariah's vision, Satan again appeared to accuse; this time with a focus on Joshua. However, the Lord rebuked Satan, and a picture of cleansing and restoration was given to the prophet: "Take off his filthy clothes … See, I have taken away your sin, and I will put rich garments on you" (Zechariah 3:4).

Let us take a cue from this revelation by rebuking Satan whenever he wants to accuse us of sin that has already been forgiven. The Word of God says that Satan's lifetime goal to circumvent God's plan for His people and undermine our confidence in His mercy, goodness, and power has failed.

DOUBT

Doubt is an unhealthy feeling of uncertainty about the truth, about facts, or about the existence of something. It paralyzes us from making quality decisions, makes us stagnant, and may keep us from being the person God has called us to be. Doubt can rob us of God's counsel and purpose for our lives.

Doubt is not having faith in God—this is a sin. We noted earlier that "without faith it is impossible to please him: for he that cometh to God must believe that he is, and that he is a rewarder of them that diligently seek Him" (Hebrews 11:6, KJV).

The enemy is so crafty that he simply sows a seed of doubt in God's people and thereby robs them of God's blessing. He has become adept at using this weapon against God's children. Disguising himself as the serpent, he sowed a seed of doubt into the mind of Eve: "Did God really say, 'You must not eat from any tree in the garden?'" (Genesis 3:1).

By causing the woman to doubt God's Word, Satan brought evil into the world. He used sin to alienate people from God.

Peter provides us with another example of doubt in action. In Matthew 14:26-31 we are presented with an account of Peter walking on water to meet Jesus. Peter began to sink as he momentarily lost his focus on Jesus and thus became overly conscious of the boisterous wind around him. We are all like Peter in some aspect of our lives. We have seen the saving hand of Jesus in our lives and witnessed first hand His miracles. Yet, when we remember certain unfinished business, we think, "Will He do this for me?" Maybe I should make a plan 'B' just in case Jesus is unwilling to meet my needs. We suddenly remember the old adage, "Heaven helps those who help themselves," and so, like father Abraham, we refuse to wait for Isaac and prematurely give birth to Ishmael. To all Peters out there, please do not allow doubt to rob you of God's best for your life.

The widow at Zarephath doubted the power of God's provision and was getting ready to cook her last meal before dying. However, Elijah then entered the scene. She momentarily thought the man of God would put bread on the table. She probably said a premature "Hallelujah!" Instead, the man of God made a demand of her. He asked her for a drink and some bread. She immediately told Elijah that all she had at present was a "handful of flour in a jar and a little oil in a jug" and to crown it all she declared, "I am gathering a few sticks to take home and make a meal for myself and my son, that we may eat it—and die" (1 Kings 17:12).

The woman had lost hope.

Undeterred by her faithless statement, Elijah encouraged the woman, "Don't be afraid. Go home and do as you have said. But first make a small cake of bread for me from what you have and bring it to me, and then make something for yourself and your son. For this is what the LORD, the God of Israel, says, 'The jar of flour will not be used up and the jug of oil will not run dry until the day the LORD gives rain on the land'" (1 Kings 17:13-14).

As a prophet, Elijah's words were the command of the Lord. The widow was asked to give all she had to sustain the man of God. She believed it and planted a portion of what she had left back into the work of God. The woman was moved from a position of doubt to one of faith. Scripture tells us that the woman obeyed God's command, and the result was marvelous in her eyes, for the Lord not only provided food for Elijah, the woman and her family on that day, but He also made provision for their future daily needs. The insignificant amount of flour and the little jug of oil fed the multitude in that household for as long as it was required. This is the result of faith and obedience. Where other children of God had deserted Him in search of prosperity, a woman realized trustful obedience to the Word of God as the only way that leads to life. Although Scripture is silent regarding what happened afterwards, I sincerely believe the woman and her family never went hungry again.

I want to assure you that God has not finished with you yet. He is still working on your behalf. However, you need to guard your spirit against doubting the Lord when faced with circumstances beyond your control.

The enemy never gives up; he will continue to test your faith in the future. To support this assertion, look at 1 Kings 17:17-18. We learn that the woman's son became ill and died. Instead of tapping into her newly found faith, the woman started to blame Elijah. She said, "What do you have against me, man of God? Did you come to remind me of my sin and kill my son?"

She forgot that God had just prospered her by making a tiny amount of flour and oil into the cornerstone of the house that fed her family for months. She also forgot God's miraculous provision and the presence of the prophet in her house. The woman began to doubt, and in her grief she allowed corrupt utterances to come out of her mouth. I can just imagine the enemy of God saying to himself, "Let's see how far your new found faith will take you when I've killed your son. Let me see if you will not blame God for your loss."

Like both Job and the widow of Zarephath, we also have a tendency to blame God when something disastrous occurs in our lives. We forget the Lord's goodness and mercy, and instead we are filled with unbelief. Some blame Him for *everything* that goes wrong, saying, "Why has God allowed so much suffering in the world?"

Do you know that experience does not necessarily lead to wisdom? The devil has had so much experience and has been practising his evil ways since the beginning of this world. Yet he has failed to learn from his past mistakes against God's children. He has forgotten that God is all-knowing and an ever-present friend in times of need. He doesn't understand that God is the Chess Master, the Skilful Tactician, the Elohim God of power and might, the Creator (Genesis 1:1), and the El Elyon (the Most High God).

Knowing what Satan was planning at Zarephath, the Lord permitted the woman's son to die so that He could show forth His awesome power and glorify himself in that situation. However, the woman's response to her son's death betrayed any recognition that "with man this is impossible, but with God all things are possible" (Matthew 19:26).

When the crisis hit, the woman started to confess her past sins and concluded that Elijah's real motive was to bring the Lord's judgment and punishment on her as opposed to bringing her a new lease of life to be treasured and guarded jealously. However, it is comforting to know that God doesn't deal with us according to our foolish utterances. Instead, He extends grace to us and allows mercy to prevail against judgment.

Elijah was strategically positioned at the widow's house for "such a time as this." Like Moses, Elijah had been fed by ravens and had seen God's miraculous hand in his life. He believed God for the miraculous resurrection of this woman's son. Was he disappointed? Initially, "Yes" (verse 20) but not for a long period. As soon as he cried to the owner of our life, "O LORD my God, let this boy's life return to him!" (1 Kings 17:21), the Bible tells us the Lord heard Elijah's cry, and the boy's life returned to him, and he lived. Praise God!

Elijah's was a very simple prayer. It was not peppered with holy language or anything to suggest that Elijah had any power of his own. He simply made a heartfelt prayer. God was not going to disappoint His obedient prophet. He honored Elijah's request and showed him off to the world, so much so that the woman could not keep it to herself anymore. She had to concede: "Now I know that you are a man of God and that the word of the LORD from your mouth is the truth" (1 Kings 17:24).

Her statement tells us that the woman had earlier entertained doubts about the validity of the prophet Elijah as a man of God.

Before you start to condemn her, permit me to say that we are all just like the widow at Zarephath. God can speak today through one of His prophets, and we'll say "I want to believe you, man of God, but I would rather contain my excitement until I see it." We would seek to defend our actions by saying, "Doesn't Scripture tell us to test every spirit (1 John 4:1)[11] and also to watch out for false prophets (Matthew 7:15)"?

The interesting thing to me is that, when God speaks through us, we sometimes feel hurt when others do not then receive it wholeheartedly. We take it as a personal rejection instead of just releasing them to the Father.

When doubt and fear come your way, don't look at the problem, instead look up to Jesus. Like doubt, fear erodes our confidence; but God's promises inspire faith and hope in us. Peter momentarily walked on water before allowing doubt to creep into his mind. But Jesus did not punish him nor allow him to drown. He saved Peter.

Let your fear drive you into the hand of Jesus, and you, too, will be delivered from the stronghold of fear and into the loving hand of Jesus. If you are still not convinced, let me conclude with a story, sent to me by e-mail, entitled "The Doubt Brought the End."

THE STORY OF A CLIFFHANGER[2]

He was determined to reach the summit of a high mountain alone because he wanted all the glory. His desire to set a new world record spurred him on to continue climbing through the day and night until overcome by darkness and zero visibility.

A few meters away from the summit, he slipped climbing a ridge and fell off, falling at frightening speed. He saw his life pass before his eyes, and in those anguishing moments he thought death was near.

Suddenly, he felt the tightening of the rope around his waist that tied him to a nail embedded in the rock wall of the mountain.

In desperation, and suspended in mid-air, our lone climber screams, "God, please help me!" According to the story, a deep voice from Heaven responded, "What would you have me do?" To which our man replied, "Save me!" The Lord then asked him, "Do you really think I can save you?" And the man replied, "Of course, my Lord!"

The Lord instructed the man, "Cut the rope." The man was silent for a moment, and then he tightened the rope around his waist. In the morning, the mountain rescue team found a man frozen to death, his hands wrapped firmly around a rope tied to his waist—hanging two feet from the ground!

You may laugh! This is supposed to be light relief from all the heavy stuff you have been reading in the previous chapters. However, the question is: "How tight are your ropes?" Would you let go when the going gets tough? Unlike the Cliffhanger, will you make a decision today to stop doubting God? Will you trust the one who declared, "For I the LORD thy God will hold thy right hand, saying unto thee, Fear not; I will help thee" (Isaiah 41:13, KJV).

The Lord had already saved our imaginary friend, the Cliffhanger. But the man doubted God and feared that God might not be willing to save him. He wondered if God's request for him to cut the rope was because God actually wanted him to die. Our man refused to enter into the finished work of Jesus. Instead, he cut himself off from God's loving hand and robbed himself of a glorious testimony that would have been the envy of his friends and enemies alike!

I can even imagine our friend making a good fortune from a book entitled *How the Lord Saved Me from Certain Death*. I can see him appearing on talk shows telling his rescue story. I can imagine the headline news: "Cliffhanger's miraculous rescue by divine hand." I can see him telling his glory-story and people flocking into his church with a desire to meet with Jesus because of his story. However, it wasn't to be, as he doubted God and was consumed with fear, and as such robbed himself of all the testimonies of the saving hand of Jesus.

As for you, there is hope if only you will believe. On the death and subsequent resurrection of Lazarus, Jesus said, "Did I not tell you that if you believed, you would see the glory of God?" (John 11:40).

Today, Jesus is saying the same to you and me. Let us come out of the spiritual shackle of fear and rise up with faith to be all that God has promised us.

End Notes

1. Murphy, Joseph. *The Power of Your Subconscious Mind*. Pocket Books, 2000.
2. Via email. author unknown.

FOUR

FEAR OF FAILURE

Unhealthy fear can be induced by negative spiritual forces and will torment people irrespective of their religious beliefs or denominational allegiance. The spirit of fear is from the devil and it uses any possible means to bring us into submission. Fear is one of Satan's instruments of command, without which he is powerless. Our enemy is a well-schooled manipulator and grade-A deceiver. Satan's followers are ruled with an iron fist, and he operates by using, among other tactics, a code of divide and rule. He uses his tenure of a relentless reign of terror and attacks to weaken our resolve to enter into God's plans and purposes for our lives.

Satan uses our failures to get us to listen to him. The degree of his relentless attack on us may give us an idea of the wonderful plan God has for our lives. This is because Satan will not generally bother to attack his obedient servants. Come to think of it, why should I attack my trusted assistants, unless they have done something wrong or there is mutiny in the camp? The only difference is that Satan likes to see everyone afraid of him so that he can use fear to control our affairs.

Scripture tells us that the fear of the Lord is the beginning of wisdom and the end of all other fears. Has it not been decreed that you shall serve no other god except the I Am? Satan is aware of all this, and he will do everything possible to make us doubt the Word of God through bowing to fear.

THE ENEMY ATTACKS WHEN YOU ARE VULNERABLE

At the beginning of Jesus' ministry on earth, Satan cornered him when He was most vulnerable and yet powerful. Jesus had just fasted for forty days and nights and was hungry (Matthew 4:1-2). Satan, ever the opportunist, reckoned that if he could stop Jesus before He walked in the full measure of the Father's authority, he would rule planet earth forever. Satan failed miserably in his attempt, as Jesus was well aware of His heritage and authority. We, too, can triumph in the face of relentless attack and temptation by remaining in our Father's will and exercising our authority as sons of the heavenly Father.

As with Adam and Eve, all Satan wanted to do was to make accusations against Jesus to the Father right then, rather than at a later date. Satan sought to discredit the Son's administration of the Father's affairs. If he had succeeded, Jesus would not have opened the physical and spiritual eyes of the blind. He would not have set the captives free and given liberty to the sons of God. He would not have healed people of sickness, disease, and various infirmities. Lazarus would have stayed dead in the tomb. And above all, Jesus' blood would not be without blemish, meaning He could not have paid the ultimate price to save mankind.

Satan forgot that he was a created being and that the manual of creation rests in the Father's palm. He (Satan) was not aware of the Father's secret weapon. His eyes were not open spiritually to see the Holy Spirit at work. He took Jesus to a very high mountain and showed Him all the kingdoms of the world and their splendor, and promised to give the joint heir to the throne what already belonged to Him. "All this I will give you," he said, "if you will bow down and worship me" (Matthew 4:9).

Jesus asserted the authority of the Word by reminding the tempter who really controls the world's affairs. Satan ought to bow down and worship God the Son, and not the other way round. Jesus, being aware of His heritage, had to use His authority. He commanded the devil, "Away from me, Satan! For it is written: 'Worship the Lord your God, and serve Him only'" (Matthew 4:10).

Jesus did not allow His current circumstances to cloud His judgment. He did not sell His birthright like Esau, as a result of hunger.

Instead He used His spiritual authority. Using today's language, He said to Satan, *"Are you kidding me? Get out of here! I cannot tolerate you any longer, as your antics are not funny! Go find some ignorant low lifes and dangle that carrot to them. Be warned, I am still coming to set them free and deliver them from your grip."*

What has this to do with the fear of failure? You see Jesus could have given up for fear that He might fail. The job was difficult, and His Father's sworn enemy was after Him. He was weak from hunger but He also was powerful from fasting and knew whose authority He wielded. Jesus was and is all-powerful, and Satan did not recognize the full extent of His divine power. We, too, must stand our ground by learning to use the Word of God against Satan's lies and not give in to fear that proceeds from the stress of temptation. Instead we must move forward in His authority.

WHAT IS FAILURE?

Before we go any further, I believe it is necessary to define failure. What is failure? According to the *Collins Gem English Dictionary & Thesaurus,* 2002 edition, "to fail is to: be unsuccessful, stop operating or working below the required standard; be insufficient, run short, be wanting when in need, defeat, downfall, miscarriage, overthrow; disappointment, incompetent, loser, no-good, non-starter."[1]

Another definition is as follows: "A failing to do or perform; a state of inability to perform a normal function adequately; heart failure—a fracturing or giving way under stress; a lack of success, etc."[2]

The above definitions tell us that we fail when we can no longer perform efficiently the task assigned to us, or when we buckle under pressure, just as a heart can give way under stress. As a result of failure, we not only disappoint ourselves but also other people who appointed us to that post. Worse still is the non-starter—the person who fails to start learning the job assigned to him because he is afraid; he has simply failed from the beginning. There is no lifeline for him because you do not fall if you do not embark upon a task. If you fail to start, you cannot take a step backward to trace the point of deviation from the original plan or find out where the plan was derailed. In my humble opinion, the person who fails to start is the person who has really failed.

The fear of failure itself creates the experience of failure. We know we want to succeed, yet we have a fear of success because if we succeed we will at some point lose that success because nothing lasts forever. One part of us tries to work hard, make all the right moves, and get that competitive edge.

Yet, at the same time another part of us is trembling with fear and doing everything possible to sabotage our own efforts. We give up just when we get close, or else we make stupid mistakes. That was why Job lamented, "What I feared has come upon me; what I dreaded has happened to me" (Job 3:25).

There is a story about a brilliant law student who had a fear of speaking in public. He always scored the highest marks in written examinations but scored below average whenever he had to role-play court appearances. His mind would go blank, his body would shake, and he was generally paralyzed with fear because he had failed in this area as a young man and his friends had done a good job of reducing his confidence level to almost zero. He worried constantly about failure, and these negative thoughts became charged with real fear so that he actually failed.

Like Job, this brilliant student was requesting his subconscious mind to see to it that he did actually fail, which is exactly what happened. In order for our student to get out of this predicament, he needed to be relaxed, peaceful, and confident. He needed to think of himself as already being successful, for "as [a man] thinketh in his heart, so is he" (Proverbs 23:7, KJV).

Our friend needed to take every thought captive and subject it to the obedience of Christ (2 Corinthians 10:5). He needed to guard his mind, be sober in his spirit, and be guided by the Holy Spirit. James says, "Submit yourselves, then, to God. Resist the devil, and he will flee from you" (James 4:7).

None of the above can be accomplished by our flesh; we need to invite the Spirit of God to help us live a victorious life.

Having discussed the effect our subconscious mind can have in achieving a particular outcome; it is time to turn our attention to the impact of other people's opinions of us. We often let the level of approval from others determine our sense of success or failure. The Bible admonishes us in Colossians 3:23-24, "Whatever you do, work at it with all your heart, as working for the Lord, not for men, since you know that you will receive an inheritance from the Lord as a reward. It is the Lord Christ you are serving."

The above passage reminds us to determine success in terms of faithfulness to God. He will reward those who diligently serve Him in any capacity, even if we have failed in the eyes of the world. Failure is subjective and cannot always be quantified in monetary terms. It is therefore only a failure if we validate it as such in our thinking, speaking, and actions. The fact that our ventures did not yield the perceived results does not make us failures. Instead we need to use our experiences positively to lead us into success.

Our God specializes in turning our weaknesses into strength as was seen in the life of Peter. Jesus rebuked Peter for not being able to keep watch for one hour in the Garden of Gethsemane. Peter failed again when he denied Jesus three times. Despite Peter's shortcomings, Jesus' plan for him was not hindered; the Church was still built on the foundation of Peter's confession of faith in Jesus as the Messiah (Matthew 16:16-18). Ephesians 2:20 also tells us that the Church is built on the foundation of the apostles and prophets as they preached and taught God's Word.

Peter's failures did not come as a surprise to Jesus. Instead of abandoning Peter, Jesus worked everything together for his good because of their mutual love and trust for one another.

PERSONAL EXPERIENCE OF FAILURE

The truth is that in some way and at some time everyone has experienced failure. In my teenage years, I failed an end-of-year examination and repeated years one and two. In year three, I was very ill with a fever during the examination period to the extent that I could not attend school, thereby missing all the revision exercises.

As I was someone who usually studied only at examination time, people already had written me off as a failure again. But God had a different plan because while on my sick bed a desire to pray came over me, and I prayed to God. I said, "If only You would rescue me from this position of defeat, I will follow You." At this time I had not known Jesus, as I was still a Muslim, entrenched in the religious world of Islam. However, I attended morning and evening chapel as it was compulsory at the school, for Christianity was the only form of spirituality on the school campus.

To my amazement, I started studying for the examination. Although the fever was still physically present, I studied on my sick bed throughout the two weeks of the examination season. Guess what? As usual, my fever and headache disappeared on the last day of the examinations, but I already had completed the tests. This was the turning point for me in defeating the spirit of sickness during examinations. I achieved the best results ever in that year, which prompted my father to check with the school authorities to ascertain the validity of my newly found excellence.

What am I saying? By the intervention of the one whom I now know as Jesus, the shackles of the examination stronghold were broken, and the bogeyman of sickness was defeated. All glory to Jesus! The world may have written you off as a failure, but if you do not write yourself off and you seek help from Master Jesus, you will smile again. He gives us more than one chance. In fact, He is always calling us saying, "My son, come to me, I have the answer to all your struggles and worries."

Hebrews 2:17-18 and 4:15-16 remind us of God's unconditional love for His children and that Jesus Christ, our high priest, entered fully into the human experience and was faced with every kind of temptation a person can have. So He knows about our trials, temptations, weaknesses, and failures. The good news is that He still loves us and has finished His work on the Cross entirely for our benefits.

I am a father of two wonderful and God-fearing boys. When they misbehave or do not perform well at school, I may be hurt or saddened by their inadequacies because of all the efforts and opportunities that have been given to them. As I have tasted failure before and know beyond a shadow of doubt that "failure is not cool," instead of despising them, I let them know that it's time to rise to the occasion. It is a time for extra study at home, time for the Saturday-school, and time for reducing those extra-curricular activities. It's time to answer the wake-up call! It is also a time to take authority in prayer over the root causes of their misbehavior or low performance.

Hence, I have corrected them in love. We work together to re-channel our focus onto what is necessary and expedient. Failure has awakened a greater tenderness and support toward my children because I have recognized my own inadequacies. In like manner, the Lord understands our weaknesses and our inadequacies; and our awareness of them also helps us to understand His marvelous grace.

At this point, let us go on a wonderful tour of Scripture in order to address this issue of fear of failure.

Scriptural Experiences of Failure and Success

In Matthew 25:14-30, with a special focus on verse 25, we are told that a wealthy man entrusted his estate to three key workers. He gave them talents of money according to their abilities. To one, he gave five talents; to the second, two talents; while the third was entrusted with only one talent. On return from his journey, the master demanded to see their profit and loss accounts. The man with five talents returned ten talents (a gain of five talents). The man with two talents also came and returned four talents (a gain of two talents). Both men received the master's acclaim and a promise to be entrusted with many things. However, the man with one talent said, "I was afraid and went out and hid your talent in the ground. See, here is what belongs to you" (Matthew 25:25).

The third servant was mistaken in his evaluation of what was important to his master, namely the expectation of a return of investment. The Scripture tells us that he was scolded, the one talent was taken away from him, and he was cast out into the wilderness.

Just to give you an idea of the kind of money squandered by the third servant, in biblical times one talent was about fifteen years' salary. This is the kind of money people are looking for today for various projects. In fact, I know of many people trying to get a business start up or business expansion loan today who have been asked by the banking institutions to bring their heart as collateral or who have mortgaged their soul to the devil via the loan sharks!

The master in this parable had given his servants an opportunity to test their skills in the marketplace; he wanted them to use their initiative and profit from their investment through the practice of good judgment. The question in my mind is: Was this servant afraid of work, pain, or afraid to serve? I could hear him saying, "Am I up to the task? Suppose I cannot do it? I do not wish to be rejected by the people who matter." The problem with the fear of failure is that it will always want us to bury our gifts, and the consequences we fear usually occur anyway because we fail to start.

The difference between underachieving people and people who excel in their endeavors in life is their attitude and response to failure.

Great people of the Bible like Moses, Gideon, Deborah, Esther, or Jeremiah had to conquer their natural fears. We, too, will conquer our fear in Jesus' name! Fear of starvation made the Israelites want to run back to Egypt. Fear of their critics or worse made the disciples forsake Jesus in His darkest hour, and it made Peter deny Him three times.

Remember the story of David and Goliath in 1 Samuel 17? Saul and his soldiers got dressed for battle every morning, only to run in fear when challenged by Goliath. They ran to their tents, a place of solace and physical safety. They ran into their comfort zone where no one would challenge their authority or readiness for battle. David, on the other hand, ran toward Goliath.

Where Saul's army saw Goliath as too big to kill, David saw Goliath as too big to miss.

I am sure that you can immediately see the difference between fear and faith! Scripture puts it this way: "As the Philistine moved closer to attack him, David ran quickly toward the battle line to meet him. Reaching into his bag and taking out a stone, he slung it and struck the Philistine on the forehead. The stone sank into his forehead, and he fell face down on the ground" (1 Samuel 17:48-49).

David had earlier warned Goliath that he was not alone in the battle, that the host of heaven was with him. Besides, it was not David's battle, "for the battle is the LORD'S" (1 Samuel 17:47). David knew something that neither Saul's army nor Goliath knew—that it is neither by might nor power but by the Spirit of the Lord (Zechariah 4:6). David knew that with the Lord in his camp victory was certain. Assured of God's covenant promise and His presence, David ran and stood over Goliath, took the sword from him, and used it to cut off the Philistine's head.

God's People, please do not hide inside your shells, for the safety zone will not bring victory. Be like David! Answer those taunting, mocking voices of failure with a cry to the Father. We need to reject what people say, in order not to reject what God is saying. Use David's formula for victory by declaring the name of Jesus. Have you forgotten that song, "At the name of Jesus, every knee shall bow, and every tongue confess that Jesus Christ is Lord"? The mention of Jesus' name empowers the host of Heaven to act, and the forces of hell tremble for they remember when He came to their camp to conquer death and won victory for all those who confess His name.

I have been exposing the causes of fear, exalting and encouraging readers from the beginning of this book. It is now time for a little counseling session, the purpose of which is to provide guidance and solutions to people suffering from the effects of failure in their lives and also to serve as a pointer for helpers.

HELPING-PEOPLE-THROUGH-FAILURE CHECKLIST

We need to work through one or more of the following.

Step 1. Try to identify the cause of the failure. Check particularly the following:

- Was the failure due to bad or inadequate planning?
- Was the failure due to lack of depth in the business strategy employed or simply due to lack of adequate marketing?
- Had the person bitten off more than he/she could chew? For example, by taking on a project beyond his/her level of expertise?
- Was it a failure to apply oneself or a result of indiscipline?
- Were incompetent staff/the wrong people employed to administer the project?
- Was the level of business advice received competent or adequate?
- Did the failure occur due to lack of knowledge or the application of a quick-fix method?

- Was the person resisting change or other factors beyond his/her control?
- Was it an act of the enemy who sneaked in to sow tares while everyone was asleep?

If feedback is frank and honest answers are provided, a lot should come out of the above analysis. If the findings are properly utilized, the probability of a breakthrough may be high especially when God is actively present in the situation.

Step 2. Allow a person to admit any shortcomings and do not invalidate his/her experience. This is because, like the unsaved, if he/she refuses to recognize any inadequacy, you cannot be of help. The feelings of failure will become repressed and form a springboard for further problems. This can take the form of depression or inactivity because the spirit of fear has taken root in his/her mind. Just as repentance is vital to salvation, so you need to give repentance opportunities to a person for his/her wrongdoing in a situation, if this has resulted in failure. It is, however, important that we encourage the person not to focus on past failures to the extent that he/she becomes paralyzed by fear.

Step 3. Encourage him/her to see the overruling providence of God. Scripture declares in Romans 8:28, "And we know that in all things God works for the good of those who love him, who have been called according to his purpose."

We need to remind the person that God is not oblivious to our failures and not helpless in the situation. God can straighten every crooked path. Remind the person about David who returned from the battlefield only to find that his family and the rest of the city had been taken captive by the Amalekites (a group of desert raiders). The whole city had been burned.

First Samuel 30 records that "David and his men wept aloud until they had no strength left to weep" (verse 4).

After this period of grief, the people turned against David. Faced with his own personal loss, the loss of the city, and being blamed by everyone, David felt like a failure but chose not to give up. We can remind the person struggling with failure about David's coping strategy. The Bible tells us, "But David found strength in the LORD his God" (verse 6).

How did David encourage himself in the Lord?

David, being a worshiper, would have worshiped the Lord until he could fully feel His presence. He would have prayed fervently for help. He would have remembered the grace of God in his life. He must have said something like this: "Lord, you are a sovereign God, a loving Father. Your love enfolds me every day, and your faithfulness is new every morning. I need your wisdom to deal with this situation, and above all I need your help."

From the throne of praise, David must have found peace and guidance. From there he must have found the courage to ask the Lord, "Shall I pursue this raiding party? Will I overtake them?" And the loving God answered through His priest Abiathar, "Pursue them . . . You will certainly overtake them and succeed in the rescue" (verse 8).

Scripture tells us that on hearing a word from the Lord, David pursued the Amalekites and came home with all the captives and a great bounty (verses 18-19. For a moment it would appear that David had been defeated, but David's principle was to be defeated and yet not surrender, and to consult with the only one who could guarantee victory. We need to include David's strategy in our defensive armor.

The above processes are of relevance to individuals, organizations, and financial institutions that specialize in counseling people who have suffered losses in their ventures. They encourage us to take stock of our plans, tactics, and strategies in order to determine areas where we are deficient. They help us to keep going and not give up an ambition or calling because of a setback.

Taking stock of our situation helps us to find better ways of running profitable and successful business ventures. It may point us in the direction of an experienced business adviser who can provide the much-needed guidance. Above all, it drives us into the arms of the Master Strategist, the Creator of Heaven and earth. Most people in business know the value of a good business or financial adviser to the success of projects, especially if this involves financial backing from the banking institutions. One is suddenly filled with renewed determination to succeed, and our renewed confidence becomes a source of inspiration to the people working with us.

Like David, anyone who has suffered business failures should not be discouraged and should definitely not be stopped from planning new ventures. Most defeats are temporary, it's only giving up that makes them permanent. Reading through an autobiography of some successful business people today, I discovered that they are only successful because of perseverance in business, good planning, and financial backing. As Christians, our first source of advice and consultation should be from the Lord, as only He gives the power to get wealth. On receiving His royal backing, we may notice we have a confidence previously unknown to us. The understanding that we have the full backing of the Most High God is satisfying and creates in us the determination to succeed.

ESSENTIAL STEPS FOR A POSITIVE OUTCOME

1. Cry to the Lord for Help

When Peter walked on water and began to sink (Matthew 14:22-33), he did not wait until fully immersed in the water but immediately cried out to the Lord for help. I believe that we should take our lead from Peter and cry out to Jesus for help when the effect of failures is about to overwhelm us. It is important to note that Jesus did not condemn Peter for his failure. He simply took Peter's hand and walked back to the boat before gently rebuking him for his mistake, saying, "You of little faith" (Matthew 14:31). This tells us that in order to live victoriously after a failure; we need to take Jesus' hand irrespective of our circumstances and problems. Notice that after Peter called out to Jesus for help, he did walk victoriously on water because Jesus simply exchanged Peter's failure for success. If you feel like crying out to Jesus now for help, please do so, for He is waiting to make himself strong in your life and to give you grace to enjoy all things (including success, wealth, joy, and such). These are things that you do not deserve but which are simply available to you by virtue of your connection and alignment with Jesus. Do not let the feelings associated with past failures paralyze your creativity and lead you into the strange world of depression.

2. Confess positively

You may have felt trapped by circumstances, unable to influence events. This may still be true for now, but you need to be fully persuaded that God is in control. Times and seasons are under His control. His plans for you are for good and not evil. He has already made provision for your success. Expect good things to happen to you and constantly banish negative thoughts with the Word of God. Avoid embracing the following three negative elements (the three 'P's).

- Powerlessness—*"I'll never be able to do this."* Instead, choose the positive version that says, "I'm tired at the moment, but I'll be able to do it after a good night's sleep." Or, say, "With man this is impossible, but with God all things are possible" (Matthew 19:26).

- Pervasiveness—*"I'm useless at everything."* This attitude and confession begins to challenge us in everything we seek to do. Change it to, "I can do everything through him who gives me strength"(Philippians 4:13).

- Personalization—*"Things like this always happen to me."* Change it to, "Surely goodness and love will follow me all the days of my life" (Psalm 23:6).

3. Put Failure Behind You

Failures come with trappings for all to see. Failure may lead to loss of status, possessions, and focus. After a failure, you need to regain your confidence by employing a positive attitude. Start with a clean sheet. Learn to deal with your disappointment and own the reason for the disappointment but do not let it paralyze you. Allow old things to pass away and let new things come in. To do this, you must begin by treating failures as a thing of the past. If you do this, a world of possibility will start to open up. Confess something like, "I used to be poor, and now I'm blessed with all the blessings in Christ Jesus." You may wish to make a list of some of the things you are currently struggling with at present, and come up with a statement that puts failure into the past. When you do this, you are forgetting things of the past and reaching out to touch new things.

4. Do Not Overlook the Simple Option

You may be faced with a difficult choice between two alternatives and unable to make a decision, or it may simply be that all the options appear impossible. Do not forget that there is always a way out—God is the wise one. You need to go to Him in prayer and ask the Holy Spirit to reveal the simple option. Listen to the guidance of the Holy Spirit and be willing to do what He says no matter how stupid it seems. Your solution is hidden in His Word.

5. Be Determined to Succeed

This is when you purpose in your heart to succeed against every circumstance and limitation. In this frame of mind, you are prepared to do whatever it takes to be successful, and you remain focused on getting back on your feet. Rest if you must, but finishing the race is the goal. In our earlier story, David rested and mourned his presumed losses, but one word from the Lord re-energized him to pursue and recover double portions.

SEEKING GOD'S PLANS FOR US

God really does work everything together for the good of those who love Him. If our friend still feels deeply condemned for the failure, perhaps suggest a medical check-up. If the doctor or counselor happens to be a Christian, so much the better. It is also important to take the person on a tour of the Bible to teach him/her what the Lord says about our failures and His good plans and thoughts for us. In 1 John 5:4-5, the Word of God calls everyone born of God an overcomer. That tells us that we all have day-by-day victory over anything the world throws our way because of our divine connection. Praise God!

At times, the very problems we think are going to destroy us become platforms for our promotion. The enemies we face often make us aware of an area of need that we may never have recognized had we not been subject to the attack. Failures led to blessing for David (1 Samuel 30). The trials and tribulations of Joseph led him to become the governor of Egypt (Genesis 41:40-44). I believe that as sons of God, failures are not final in our lives. Adversity is nothing more than an incubator to process the destiny of men and women who will change the course of history.

We need to remember that our failures do not surprise God. In fact that is one of the reasons He gave His Son Jesus Christ—to pay the debt of our physical, spiritual, and financial failures. He brought us back into full fellowship with the Father, and the wonder of the gospel is that our failures revealed God's greatest success (1 John 2:1-2). Neither do our failures determine our identity or worth. God has adopted us as His children; therefore our identity and worth are in Him. He uses failure to train us, reveal His love, and shape us into holiness. I would like readers to remember that the man who does not make mistakes is unlikely to make anything at all. Failure is an opportunity to excel, as we learn lessons after a disappointment. When a door closes on something you fervently believe in or an opportunity you hate to lose, do not just walk away from it. Step back, consult God, and ask Him, "Is this door really closed?"

Like David, we should check whether there is something we can do (or stop doing) to keep the door open. Ask God, "Shall I pursue them? Will I overtake them?" Ask for the master key to unlock the door that was previously shut; but use the precious master key wisely to ensure that you are unlocking the correct door assigned to you by the Father.

Rev. George Adegboye in his book *Handling the Opposite* said, "It is not the number of times that you fall that determines who you become; it is what you do when you fall. How do you keep on living when you fall? How do you keep on living when what you value most may have been taken from you? How do you start all over again?"

These are very important questions, and there are no one-size-fits-all answers. I can assure you that it does not matter how many times you fail. The Lord can still open the right door for you, and one success will open the doors for future successes. Remember, you are an overcomer; and, if you remain in Jesus, He is more than able to exchange your failure for success.

To quote the encouraging words of Wess Roberts, the author of *Leadership Secrets of Attila the Hun,* "My book was turned down by seventeen publishers, but I had put so much work into it that I could not just let it die. I went ahead and had copies of it printed up at my own expense and eventually, by word of mouth, there was enough interest in it that I could no longer handle orders efficiently. Warner Books bought the rights, and it went on to become one of the top ten best-selling titles for the year. Had I just been discouraged and thrown it over, the whole thing never would have come to fruition."

Thomas Edison said, "Of the two hundred light bulbs that didn't work, every failure told me something that I was able to incorporate into the next attempt."

Rev. Nigel Armstrong said, "Most defeats are temporary, and only become permanent when you give up hope of recovery" In his wisdom, the same Rev Armstrong said, "Reject what people say, in order not to reject what God is saying." Very wise words!

Rev. George Adegboye, Rev. Nigel Armstrong, Wess Roberts, and Thomas Edison understood that failures and false starts are a precondition of success and that failure is not a dead end. In Christ, failure becomes the doorway to lasting change. We may want to ask ourselves the following questions:

- What have I settled for?
- Have I given up on things that really matter?
- Have I compromised on things that really matter to me rather than learning a new way to go about things?
- What do I really want?
- If I knew I could not fail, what would I do?

My family in Christ, if we can provide honest answers to the above questions and make the necessary adjustment as directed by the Holy Spirit, we will begin to receive new vision for our future—the type that will profit and assure us of success. Let us cast our minds back to Paul's account of his remarkable experience in 2 Corinthians 12, where he pleaded with God to remove his thorn three times, and the answer came: "My grace is sufficient for you, for my power is made perfect in weakness" (2 Corinthians 12:9).

In this passage, the Lord is telling Paul that He allowed the tormentor to attack him because He wanted to use Paul's light affliction to strengthen him. Note that it is the spirit of Paul that is the object of divine strengthening at the expense of the affliction of the flesh in its carnality. It is also important to know that our weaknesses provide the ideal opportunity for God to manifest His divine power in other aspects of our lives and personalities. To put it simply, Paul was encouraging us to give our failures to the Lord and watch Him turn them into uncommon blessings.

Paul Arden in his book, *It's Not How Good You Are, It's How Good You Want to Be*, tells a story that strengthened me to continue writing this book at a time when it all seemed too much for me. The story is about the making of the film *Citizen Kane*. Apparently the producer, Orson Wells, could not find any backers, but he did raise a small sum for casting. Afterwards he begged, borrowed, and cajoled people into building sets and shooting full-blown screen tests that eventually formed a third of the film. At this time backers could see what they were getting, and he got the much-needed money to complete the film. If Orson Wells had listened to all the negative opinions and the experts of impossibilities, the film would be just another concept in the endless list of ideas that never happened.

The above story encourages me to feel the fear but do it anyway. It tells me that if I am fully persuaded that my heart is positively stirred toward a project, I should not allow negative opinions from earthly experts to sabotage my dreams, nor let previous disappointments discourage me from following the leading of the Holy Spirit. If the first idea did not work, please just go back to the drawing board like a worthwhile architect and make the necessary adjustments, then try again.

Persistence yield dividends. Our God had to go back to the drawing board and by His salvation plan redesign our whole being, so that when we become born again, the old self is gone and behold new things have arrived. It took the sacrifice of Jesus on the Cross to redeem mankind.

Do not take "No" for an answer. Redesign, remodel, and repackage if you have to, but do not give up, because if you don't do it, it doesn't exist.

Patience and faith are twin virtues necessary during the rebuilding process. Patience enables you to wait for God's plan and timing, but faith releases in you the desire to believe and appropriate it. According to Hebrews 10:35-36, when patience is combined with obedience we are released onto the path of success and given the ability to enter into God's promise.

To balance the above, however, it is good practice to invite trusted people to comment on our ideas. Instead of seeking approval, we may want to ask questions like "What do you see wrong with it?" or "How can I improve upon it?" Using this approach enables us to receive truthful and critical answers, which may assist us in improving our ideas or products. Brothers and Sisters, let us not allow fear, negative opinions, or intimidation prevent us from fulfilling God's purpose for our lives.

I would like to share with you the following parable, told by Henri Nouwen when he addressed the Presbyterian Peace Fellowship Breakfast at the General Assembly in Indianapolis, Indiana, on June, 1985.[3]

Light Relief to a Rather Consuming Topic

A group of people surveyed the resources of the world, and they said to each other, "How can we be sure that we will have enough in hard times? We want to survive whatever happens. Let us start collecting food, materials, and knowledge so that we are safe and secure when a crisis occurs." So these fearful people started hoarding, so much that other people protested and said, "Hey, you have much more than you need, while we don't have enough to survive. Give us part of your wealth."

The fearful hoarders said, "No, no, no, we need to keep this in case of emergencies, in case things go bad for us, too, in case our lives are threatened." But the others said, "We are dying now. Please give us food and materials and knowledge to survive. We can't wait! We need it now!"

The fearful hoarders became still more fearful, as they became afraid that the poor and hungry would attack them. So they said to one another, "Let us build walls around our wealth so that no stranger can take it away from us."

And as their fear increased they told each other, "Our enemies have become so numerous that they may be able to tear down our walls. We need to put bombs on top of the walls so that nobody would dare to even come close to us."

But instead of feeling safe and secure behind their armed walls, they found themselves trapped in the prison they had built with their own fear. They even became afraid of their own bombs, wondering if they might harm themselves more than their enemy. And gradually they came to realize that their fear of death had brought them closer to it.

These people feared failure and had forgotten that "He who dwells in the shelter of the Most High will rest in the shadow of the Almighty" (Psalm 91:1). They had put their hopes in their mountains of food reserves. Their protection was based on the prison they had built with their own hands. To make matters worse, the bomb that almost killed them was actually their secret weapon. They trusted in the work of their hands instead of taking refuge inside the fortress of God. Despite their mistrust, the Lord opened their eyes to see that the fear of failure had brought them closer to it. It just goes to show that our God is merciful and graceful. Praise be to Him!

Song of the Bird

This is another e-mailed story. A man found an eagle's egg and put it in the nest of a barnyard hen. The eagle hatched with the brood of chicks and grew up with them. All his life, the eagle did what the barnyard chicks did, thinking he was a barnyard chicken. He scratched the earth for worms and insects. He clucked and cackled. At times, he would thrash his wings and fly a few feet in the air.

Years passed, and the eagle grew very old. One day he saw a magnificent bird above him in the cloudless sky. It glided in graceful majesty among powerful wind currents with scarcely a beat of its strong golden wings. The old eagle looked up in awe. "Who is that?" he asked. "That's the eagle, the king of the birds," said his neighbor. "He belongs to the sky. We belong to the earth, we are chickens." The story ends by sadly telling us that the eagle lived and died a chicken, for that's what he thought he was.

In all honesty, I cried inwardly after reading this story because I sometimes behave like the eagle in our story, thinking, "I cannot do it, Lord! Are you sure you have called the right man to write this book?" Or like Moses, I think that I cannot speak and am not eloquent enough, instead of simply saying, "Yes, Lord, I will do it as you equip me for the job."

Going back to our story, I wondered what could have happened if only someone had enlightened our old eagle. Is it possible that he could have decided to rise up with eagle's wings and conquer the sky for the rest of his life? Brothers and Sisters in Christ, consider this as a call to rise up and be all that God has purposed for you! We ought to live as heads and not as tails; above and not below. We are more than conquerors! Let not the enemy keep us down because of past failures, bad experiences, or ignorance about who we are in Christ Jesus. As a man thinketh, so is he. Stop living like a chicken and rise up with eagle's wings.

SPIRITUAL SUCCESS

Biblically speaking, success is based on faithfulness toward God and not on results as defined by the world. Success comes as fulfilment and as a favourable outcome to our God-given vision and endeavors. People may look at us with worldly eyes, but God is Spirit and as such His work should be viewed with spiritual eyes. Everything we are or have belongs to God and not to us. Beloved, begin to see people as God sees them. Let us see ourselves with God's eyes. Remember that success is a journey and not a destination because to be really successful one has to continue repeating the success strategies while also adapting to changes in our environment.

Success is a state of mind. One can feel or see success. One must think success, as what you see in the spiritual is what you will birth in the physical. Do not let anyone tie you down with negativity. It is time to rise up with wings like an eagle and glide above all human limitations.

Fearful people are afraid to work, afraid to serve, and afraid to fail. People of faith always have someone to trust, someone to look to for help, with nothing to lose and nothing to fear.

When we have failed, God has a wonderful way of restoring us. Instead of saying "I told you so," He simply overlooks our shortcomings and tells us, "Try again. But this time do it my way." Often we wrongly assume that something is not God's will because we failed in it the first time. However it is quite possible that we failed because we acted in our own strength or because of the work of the enemy who sneaks in at night to put tares in our crops.

We need to remember that there is no instant solution as the only way to learn is through guidance, experience and mistakes.

It is important to know that nothing is impossible for God and that He has a way of getting us out of every trouble. After Peter and his friends toiled all night and caught nothing, Jesus came onto the scene and gave them divine direction. As a result of their obedience, the fishermen had a bountiful harvest. Jesus confounded the fishing experts because He created a harvest in an area known to all human experts to be a dead end. He says, "I am the Creator of all things, and all things are subject to my instructions. I am the only one who can make a way where there appears to be no way." One word from Jesus can make a difference between failure and success. Jesus is well aware of our shortcomings, and He sometimes allows us to fail so that we may learn from our failures and discover the difference He can make in our lives.

If you could not remember anything at all from this chapter of the book, may I enjoin you to remember this: *The greatest glory story is not found in instant success but in the ability to rise up each time we fail to achieve success.*

We need to use failure as a catalyst for success and not allow people's opinions to cloud our judgment. Failure is a subjective concept. Remember that when you are peaceful, happy, joyous, and doing what you love, you are successful!

Points to Note About Success

• To be successful, you must find a problem that you are created to solve, work at finding a solution, and excel at it.

• Failure and false starts are a precondition and a major contributor to success.

• It doesn't matter how many times you fail; all you need is one success (Arthur Pine with Julie Houston).

- Most defeats are temporary; it's only giving up that makes them permanent (Nigel Armstrong)
- You must find fulfilment in whatever you are doing. Otherwise the success will be artificial, and there will be a feeling of failure incubating inside.
- A successful person has a creative mind and a clear vision of the journey's destination. He is at peace with his plans even if nothing seems to be working and no one else subscribes to his vision.
- Successful people are comfortable in their own company and certain in the company of others. That is, they are happy with who God has made them, as you cannot love others if you do not love yourself.
- To be successful, you must stop accepting false beliefs, opinions, and fears that tell you millions of reasons why your project or business ideas cannot succeed.
- Reject what people say, in order not to reject what God is saying. (Nigel Armstrong).
- Do not allow pride and laziness to lead you to the doorstep of failure. The lazy man is too proud to work, and the proud man too lazy to rest.
- The difference between underachieving people and people who excel in their endeavors in life is their attitude and response to failure.
- To become a champion, fight one more round. (James Corbett).
- People who are conventionally clever get jobs on their qualifications (the past), not on their desire to succeed (the future). (Paul Arden).
- Whether you think you can or can't, you are usually right. (Henry Ford).
- Give away everything you know, and more will come back to you. (Paul Arden).
- Success is going from failure to failure with no loss of enthusiasm. (Winston Churchill).

BIBLE VERSES TO HELP US

1. "The sluggard says, 'There is a lion outside!' or, 'I will be murdered in the streets'" (Proverbs 22:13)!
2. "For though a righteous man falls seven times, he rises again, but the wicked are brought down by calamity" (Proverbs 24:16).
3. "The steps of a (good) man are directed and established by the Lord when He delights in his way (and He busies Himself with his every step). Though he falls, he shall not be utterly cast down, for the Lord grasps his hand in support and upholds him" (Psalm 37:23-24, Amplified Version).
4. "Whatever you do, work at it with all your heart, as working for the Lord, not for men, since you know that you will receive an inheritance from the Lord as a reward. It is the Lord Christ you are serving" (Colossians 3:23-24).
5. "I was afraid and went out and hid your talent in the ground" (Matthew 25:25).
6. "And we know that in all things God works for the good of those who love him, who have been called according to his purpose" (Romans 8:28).
7. "'Pursue them,' he answered. 'You will certainly overtake them and succeed in rescue'" (1 Samuel 30:8).
8. "What I feared has come upon me; what I dreaded has happened to me. I have no peace, no quietness; I have no rest, but only turmoil" (Job 3:25-26).
9. "Do not gloat over me, my enemy! Though I have fallen, I will rise. Though I sit in darkness, the LORD will be my light" (Micah 7:8).
10. "Trust in the LORD with all your heart and lean not on your own understanding; in all your ways acknowledge him, and he will make your paths straight" (Proverbs 3:5-6).
11. "'For I know the plans I have for you,' declares the LORD, 'plans to prosper you and not to harm you, plans to give you hope and a future'" (Jeremiah 29:11).
12. "Unless the LORD builds the house, its builders labor in vain. Unless the LORD watches over the city, the watchmen stand guard in vain. In vain you rise early and stay up late, toiling for

food to eat—for he grants sleep to those he loves" (Psalm 127:1-2).

13. "Charm is deceptive, and beauty is fleeting; but a woman who fears the LORD is to be praised. Give her the reward she has earned, and let her works bring her praise at the city gate" (Proverbs 31:30-31).

14. "So do not throw away your confidence; it will be richly rewarded. You need to persevere so that when you have done the will of God, you will receive what he has promised" (Hebrews 10:35-36).

END NOTES

1. *Collins Gem English Dictionary & Thesaurus*. William Collins Sons & Co., Ltd., 2002.

2. *Franklin, Merriam-Webster, Speaking Dictionary & Thesaurus MWS-1840*. Franklin Electronic Publishers.

3. Nouwen, Henri. "Whistling in the Wilderness," address to the Presbyterian Peace Fellowship Breakfast at the General Assembly in Indianapolis, Indiana, on June, 1985.

FIVE

Fear of Death

"Blessed are the dead who die in the Lord from now on." "Yes," says the Spirit, "that they may rest from their labors, and their works follow them." (Revelation 14:13, NKJV)

Death is not a popular topic, but nevertheless a fact of life in our degenerated world. It can be expected as a result of sudden sickness or long-term illness. It can be the result of sudden organ failure or connected with an accident causing the immediate termination of life as we know it. Yet it remains a source of secret concern to us. It has become a taboo subject, and the fear of it is often repressed. The reason we do not normally talk about death is that we have not learned to look at death through God's eyes.

We are completely distraught in the face of death as though an absolutely intolerable event has occurred. The attitude of Jesus upon hearing about the death of one of His closest friends is a good pointer. Although He stayed away during the commotion period, yet Jesus was neither insensitive nor cold-hearted. Rather, the Bible asserts that He could become "deeply moved in spirit and troubled" (John 11:33). He eventually raised Lazarus from the dead, an experience that shows His mastery over death.

Perhaps we have failed to fully recognize that Jesus tasted death for every man (Hebrews 2:9) and that by His death He destroyed the devil (who used to hold the power of death) and freed those who are held in slavery by the fear of death (Hebrews 2:14-15).

The most striking thing is that death can pass off in the world as quietly as if it were nothing; whereas every other loss—an arm, a leg, money, or a job—is bound to be noticed. God has appointed the time for each person's death, and man cannot influence when it will occur. Nothing can be taken from this life when a person dies, and his exit is like his entrance (Ecclesiastes 5:15-16). However, our opening passage speaks a blessing over all those who die in the Lord. It also distinguishes clearly the type of death that occurs within God's plan, from the one which occurs without. That gives me a reason to rejoice!

What Is Death?

In ordinary terms, death is the negation of life in its proper sphere and the symbol of alienation from our loved ones. But Christ has used His own death to deliver men from the sting of death. Jesus died so that we may live, but He also conquered death by rising again from the dead. He has ascended to Heaven and will one day return in glory, as Lord, King and Judge.

The word *death* means different things to different people. For our grandparents, death was deemed to take place when the heart had ceased to beat and the lungs to breathe. However in today's world, and due to medical advancement, breathing and body nourishment can be artificially sustained even after the brain has died. Dying nowadays is in many ways more gruesome, more lonely, mechanical, and dehumanised. At times, it may be very difficult to determine technically when the moment of death has occurred. However, in practical terms, a moment must be decided upon as doctors need to be able to sign death certificates. Unless, of course, the person is presumed dead because they have been missing for a long period.

Criteria Used to Ascertain When Someone Is Dead

In his book, *The Family Medical Reference Book,*[1] Consultant-Editor Philip Evans of Guy's Hospital, London, explains the several criteria by which a general surgeon or physician will ascertain when a person is dead.

- The first is the absence of a heartbeat, examined by feeling for a pulse and listening for heart sounds in the chest.
- The second involves determining whether breathing has stopped by listening at different points on the chest for characteristic breath sounds.
- The third involves examining the surface of the eyes to see if they have a glazed appearance, usually caused by the evaporation of water from the surface of unblinking eyes.
- The fourth criterion is dilated pupils. However, it is worth noting that dilated pupils may also be seen in some types of brain injury or after an overdose of some drugs.
- The fifth criterion is pallor or blueness of the body, as a result of the tissues using up the oxygen in the blood and the redistribution of the blood by gravity to the lower parts of the body.
- The sixth criterion of death is coldness of the skin. However, climate, clothing, and physical build can all maintain the core body temperature, which may not fall drastically until some time after death unless the person died of cold.

However, a neurosurgeon (those who perform surgery on the nervous system) or a transplant surgeon may use a separate and detailed criteria of death. These criteria include loss of reflexes, clinical evidence of irrecoverable brain damage, and complete absence of any signs of consciousness. These additional tests are used to ensure the person's organs are really dead, as the fear of being buried while still alive is widespread, and the legal implications could be crippling both financially and professionally. There have been such cases of death being pronounced, usually following drug overdose and exposure to extreme cold. Likewise, there are cases of drunkards who have suffered prolonged exposure to cold and appeared dead but who actually survived.

I believe we can all see why it can be difficult to declare someone dead before proper and rigorous testing has taken place. It is not my intention to stray into the medical aspects of death, but I believe that the above will be useful for most of us who are from non-medical backgrounds. More importantly, the above sheds some light on the processes of physical death, which are inescapable to mankind.

REACTION PHASES TO THE NEWS OF IMPENDING DEATH

1. Denial and Isolation

In this phase we are unable to face the sad fact that death knocks at our door. Most of us will go through this stage, which may last between seconds and many months.

2. Anger

This is when we cannot comprehend the fact that we are dying and react in anger at people and God for allowing such a dreadful thing to happen to us.

3. Bargaining

Like children, when we cannot get our way, we suddenly think maybe we can succeed in striking some sort of bargain to postpone the inevitable from happening. Perhaps we have read about King Hezekiah's illness in the Bible and how he appealed to God. The result was that fifteen years were added to his life (2 Kings 20:1-7). We also think we may be able to use Hezekiah's strategy to change our circumstances by bargaining with God.

4. Depression

When all the above methods have failed, a person facing death is no longer able to deny the inevitable, especially when forced to undergo more surgery or hospitalization. When he cannot smile it off anymore, his anger and rage are soon replaced with a sense of great loss. He becomes depressed due to his inability to function properly and for his impending loss.

5. Acceptance

When the dying person has been given some help in working through the above phases, he will usually reach a stage during which he is neither depressed nor angry about his fate. This is when he has come to accept the inevitable.

From the above five phases I can safely say that our attitude (as family, helpers, counselors, doctors, and pastors) rather than our words will go a long way toward either helping the dying person to accept the inevitable or helping him/her to stay in denial. The importance of a doctor and/or counselors who can sit and listen cannot be underestimated as they can encourage the dying person to express innermost feelings without resentment or fear.

If the dying person is a Christian believer and in the bargaining phase, there is nothing to prevent us from standing with him/her in prayer as we know that nothing is impossible for God. If God did it for King Hezekiah, surely He can do it for our loved one because He is the same yesterday, today, and forever. Many of us have either known or heard of people being given days to live who are then miraculously healed by God. Are we helping the person to reinforce his/her denial in this? I think not.

There is a saying—"Attitude affects altitude." If the so-called dying person has the willpower to fight and/or believes that God will save him/her from an early departure from this world, his or her faith should not be met with contempt. I am sure that many experienced doctors would support the claim that some patients have survived ailments without a medical explanation as to how or why they have cheated death. This is the God factor and should not be ignored.

The Biblical Concept of Death

Earlier in this chapter, I mentioned that the word *death* means different things to different people. From one viewpoint, death is the most natural thing in the world as it is appointed that all men will die once (Hebrews 9:27). Yet from another viewpoint, death is the most unnatural of things as God's original intention for mankind was eternal life (Romans 6:23). Romans 5:12-13 tells us that such death is the result of sin and that people begin life with a sinful nature and are involved in the sin of someone else, namely Adam.

In Genesis 3, death acts as punishment for the sins of mankind. In the New Testament, Romans 6:23 states, "The wages of sin is death." However one special death, that of Jesus, cancels every claim made concerning our guilt and the guilt of the first Adam. Ultimately, death is robbed of its power, and its elimination is anticipated in Hosea 13:14: "I will ransom them from the power of the grave; I will redeem them from death. Where, O death, are your plagues? Where, O grave, is your destruction?"

Here we have a promise of redemption from death, which Paul attributes to the resurrection of Jesus Christ bringing us total victory over sin, condemnation, death, and the grave (1 Corinthians 15:55).

Some of us fear death, irrespective of our belief system. Christians know the biblical approach to death. We know that our salvation takes care of the past, present, and future and that we have been sanctified by the cleansing blood of the Lamb. By faith we believe in eternal life. We also believe in the glorification that comes to a Christian at death and afterward. Yet we are still afraid of death.

In Psalm 30 the psalmist celebrates life by giving thanks to the Lord for restoring him to perfect health and bringing him back from the brink of death. He obviously feared for his life, but he let his fears turn him toward God. We later see him pray in complete reliance on God's grace (verses 8-10). In this Psalm we see a concept of death developing where *depths* and *pit* are linked with the grave. Death is not a natural concept to us as we were created to live in an everlasting relationship with God. It was never part of the original plan but entered our world through the sin of Adam and Eve.

In Deuteronomy 30:19-20, Moses uses similar imagery when he calls upon the Israelites to choose between life and death. He reminds them that the Lord is their life. He assures them that if they choose the Lord, they effectively choose life and its benefits; any other choice leads only to eternal death. However the Lord makes it clear in Ezekiel 18:30-32 that He does not desire death for anyone. Instead of death, He calls for us to repent and live.

This powerful imagery of death carries over into the New Testament. Paul compares the result of our baptism into Christ through faith in Jesus with the result of our union with Adam through natural birth. Paul goes on to say that as we fell into sin and became subject to death in our father Adam, so we now have died and been raised again with Christ as a result of our faith in His death, burial, and resurrection as symbolized by water baptism. Peter also tells us about the redemptive work of Jesus on the Cross. He reminds us that, as a result of Christ's death on the Cross, believers are positively dead to sin so that we may live new lives and present ourselves to God as instruments of righteousness (1 Peter 2:24).

What About Physical Death?

Physical death seems inescapable. Yet Adam did not die physically on the twenty-four-hour day that he disobeyed God. He however died within the symbolic day of 1,000 years at the age of 930 years (2 Peter 3:8). It is important at this stage to establish that possession of eternal life does not cancel our physical death. Also that death, which is the result of sin, is more than bodily death.

Man does not die as a body but in the totality of his being. He dies as a spiritual and physical being. He is then awakened to start a new life, to either eternal life or to eternal condemnation. Your destination is dependent upon your choice. What are you going to choose today?

Ecclesiastes 12:7 states, "The dust returns to the ground it came from, and the spirit returns to God who gave it."

This tells us that sooner or later every one of us will die and that no one can elude death except those caught up in the rapture (1 Thessalonians 4:17). The above passage also reminds us of the reason for a relationship with the Father, as physical death leads to the separation of soul and body. The body returns to dust, while the spirit returns to God for judgment.

The good news is that Jesus assures us Christians that when we die, though our body goes to the grave, our soul is immediately with Him. That is why He declared to one of the thieves who received salvation on the Cross, "I tell you the truth, today you will be with me in paradise" (Luke 23:43).

Acts 7:54-60 tell us the story of Stephen. He was persecuted and stoned to death for rebuking the religious mob of Israel, and his soul was immediately sent into the presence of Jesus. Just as Stephen was welcomed safely home, all believers in Christ who have passed through the valley of the shadow of death will also awaken to a glorious welcome from the host of Heaven. To be absent from the body is to be present with the Lord.

This assures us Christians that death is not something to fear, as we immediately leave behind this carnal world and enter into the court of God, a place of unspoiled fellowship with the Lord.

Do I hear you ask, "Am I to expect death?" My answer is both yes and no. It is yes, because we must always be prepared for it to come without warning, except for those to whom the Lord has given prior warning. C.S. Lewis said, "If we really believe what we say we believe—if we really think that home is elsewhere and that this life is a 'wandering to find home,' why should we not look forward to the arrival?"

According to Lewis' brother, a week before his death C.S. Lewis said, "I have done all that I was sent into the world to do, and I am ready to go." I have never seen death looked on with such tranquility.

Sigmund Freud—in a 1914 paper entitled "Thoughts for the Times on War and Death"—said, "If you want to endure life, prepare yourself for death." This is probably one of the few areas where Lewis and Freud agreed. However, both statements show that they had a good grasp of the issue of death. The only difference is that Freud had an unhealthy fixation with death and was very fearful in his expectation, while Lewis, since his conversion, looked joyfully ahead to the time when he would meet with Jesus.

I am not suggesting that we are to have an unhealthy fixation with death like Freud. Neither am I suggesting that we should throw ourselves into a potentially life-threatening situation to conquer and master it so we can boast that we have cheated death. To do this would be just another form of denial of our own mortality. Instead, I am suggesting that we should make a special effort to contemplate our own death, to deal with the anxieties surrounding the realities of our own death, and to help others familiarize themselves with these concepts. Finally, I am suggesting that we should let these thoughts help us to consider our human frailties and God's supremacy to the extent that we are driven into the loving arms of our Creator, the one who is life and who has the ultimate power over death. This person is no other than Jesus.

However, I also say no, we should not expect death, because we are not simply to do nothing with our lives and stop living for fear that death could knock at anytime. We need to live fully every moment so that we may declare, like Lewis, that we have done all that we were sent into the world to do and are ready to go.

As sons of God, offspring of the mighty Father, we did not receive a spirit that makes us a slave again to fear (Romans 8:15). Once we are aware of our position in Christ Jesus, we need fear death no longer. Jesus was victorious over death by His resurrection, and as sons of God, His victory becomes ours because His purpose is to give us abundant life. The truth is that some of us still act as if we fear death, and our actions speak louder than our lip service.

At times, we behave only slightly differently from atheists and agnostics. We mourn so much that it appears to onlookers that death is the end of all hope. We have forgotten that physical death is not the end; it is but a stage in life and the door to eternal life for those who believe in Jesus Christ (John 3:16). Non-Christians should be the ones doing all the crying because they cannot transform their mansions and the wealth of this world into their next phase of life. Some people see death as the inevitable end to a gloomy and pessimistic existence. Death equals extinction and, though dreaded and feared, provides a way out. Christians, on the other hand, are like travelers who are assured of a glorious and eternal accommodation at the end of their journey.

Jesus shared in our humanity so that by His death He might destroy him who holds the power of death (Hebrews 2:14). He won the war 2,000 years ago, became victorious, and set all the captives free. By virtue of His finished work, the promise of John 3:16 was fulfilled: "For God so loved the world that He gave his one and only Son, that whoever believes in him shall not perish but have eternal life."

We are assured that we have eternal life through the finished work of Jesus on the Cross. Those who need to fear death are the ones who fail to obey Him. In contrast, those who listen to His message and believe in God who sent Him are guaranteed eternal life and have already passed from death to life (John 5:24).

By passing on to the next life, our loved ones have changed their physical and geographical location. But the knowledge that those who are in Christ Jesus are not dead but asleep and now living in a peaceful place should bring a smile to the faces of those of us left behind. The person may have been the household breadwinner or a close confidant or counselor, but we need to believe and understand that God is the Father of all fathers and will fill the vacuum left by them if only we allow Him.

Jesus' love for us is so deep that nothing, not even death, can separate us from Him. Our fears for today, our worries about tomorrow—even the powers of hell—cannot keep God's love away (Romans 8:37-39). This is not an attitude of foolish avoidance of the issue of death; rather it is recognition of the sovereignty of the covenant of God despite the grim fact of death.

Christians have a secret that ought to be shared with unbelieving friends, families, and colleagues. We need to make them aware that "Not all of us will die, but we will all be transformed" (1 Corinthians 15:51, New Living Bible).

That glorious event will happen in a moment, in the blinking of an eye, when the last trumpet is blown. At this time, Christians who have died will be raised with transformed bodies and those who are still living will be transformed so that they will never die (1 Corinthians 15:51-55). When this happens, Scripture will be fulfilled so that we can make a mockery of death saying, "O death, where is your victory? O death, where is your sting?" (1 Corinthians 15:55, New Living Bible).

Let us cast our minds to Moses. He died and was buried many years before Jesus. But the disciples recognized him when he appeared on the mountain with Jesus and Elijah, even though they had never seen him and even though, as far as we know, his body was still in the grave (Mark 9:2-8). When we die, we can expect to recognize our loved ones and other Christians, even though their bodies are still in the grave. At this time we will be like the angels and will no longer conform to the present earthly laws. In the new age there will be no more procreation and no more death (Luke 20:36).

The Apostle Paul tells a great truth to the Philippians when he declares that Christ is the source and secret of his continual joy (even in prison). He specifies that the gain brought by death is "being with Christ" and that neither power nor wealth are good motivations for living if there is no personal relationship with Christ (Philippians 1:21-23). This encourages us to focus on ensuring we have a right relationship with Christ, rather than focusing on the timing of or temporary loss caused by death.

Jesus became flesh, fought and won victory over death, and by so doing delivered those who have lived their lives as slaves to the fear of dying.

James, Jesus' brother, warns us of the danger of planning or doing business without recognizing our own mortality. He puts it like this: "Now listen, you who say, 'Today or tomorrow we will go to this or that city, spend a year there, carry on business and make money.' Why, you do not even know what will happen tomorrow. What is your life? You are a mist that appears for a little while and then vanishes. Instead, you ought to say, 'If it is the Lord's will, we will live and do this or that'" (James 4:13-15).

James is opening our minds to spiritual wisdom not taught in any business school—the wisdom that comes only from above. He has nothing against us planning for growth, change, and other projects or to reach targets at work. But he asks us to look at our lives and plan for eternity with God. If we are yet to enter into a relationship with Christ by turning away from sin and the condemnation of death into life, we should not delay our decision another day. Remember that in the blinking of an eye, when the trumpet is blown, everyone will face judgment; and the location where we spend eternity is dependent on the decision we made in this life. On that day, it will be too late to change.

According to Revelation 20:11-15, when all are gathered by the great White Throne, the books will be opened, and the dead will be judged according to the things written in it and according to what they have done. The dead (both in the sea and the grave) will be judged, and anyone whose name not found recorded in the Book of Life will be thrown into the lake of fire. *Are you sure of your salvation?*

HELPING OTHERS

We should not hesitate to introduce or discuss death when appropriate. It should not be a topic introduced only when someone actually dies or reserved exclusively for a funeral service. Learning something about it today may assist us in the future to face up to our immortality and possibly to help people in their last hour.

Some people may be uncomfortable with this teaching, but death is a fact of life. Others may be unwilling to introduce the topic of death either to the living or to those near the point of death because they themselves are uncomfortable with it. The most important thing is that friends, relatives, helpers, and counselors are sensitive to the Holy Spirit's leading in any given circumstance.

We must be aware of people's feelings and be prepared for their reactions. Dying people may be angry or in denial about their approaching death. As a result, counselors may not want to add to their internal turmoil by introducing the topic at such a time. However, we must be aware that the person may not want to force the topic into conversation themselves but would perhaps discuss it if it were introduced by the other party. We need discernment. We must not willingly shy away from the discussion when those seeking counseling are willing to learn more about the one element of life that is almost certain to occur.

Should the counselor introduce the topic when counseling the dying and the grieving? If handled with tact, sensitivity, perceptiveness, and in good taste, those seeking counseling would probably find some measure of comfort from the discussion. To introduce the topic could help to eliminate some of the mental suffering and grief associated with death and dying.

If the person has accepted Jesus as Lord and Savior, we need to let him or her know that Heaven is a place of no pain and no disease or sickness and that eternity with unbroken relationship with the Father awaits us. However, if the person does not know Jesus and has not submitted to the lordship of Christ, we should introduce him or her to the person of Jesus Christ and the good news of salvation. It is important that we exercise good judgment in this endeavor as to the proper timing and appropriateness for the individual. Above all, counselors should allow the Spirit of the Lord to be their source of guidance in this as in all things.

CHRISTIAN DEATH

"Brothers, we do not want you to be ignorant about those who fall asleep, or to grieve like the rest of men, who have no hope" (1 Thessalonians 4:13).

For many people death is shrouded in mystery. Literature shows that first-century pagans viewed death with horror, as the end of everything. The Christian attitude should be in total contrast because for Christians sleep is a particular metaphor for death, since death's finality and horror are removed by the assurance of resurrection.

It is important to reinforce our understanding that those who die in the Lord are blessed because they are welcomed by the saints and taken into the Lord's presence, a place of uninterrupted fellowship with Jesus for eternity. However, it is sad to know that despite our belief in glorification at death and afterwards, we are not too dissimilar to non-Christian in terms of our fear of death.

According to Robin Wakely[2], F.W.H. Myers once asked his church warden what he thought would happen to him at death. The church warden gave a typical Christian answer: "I shall immediately depart unto everlasting felicity." Yet, this was followed by his true state of mind as he continued, "But I do wish you would not talk about such unpleasant subjects!" To put it simply, he feared that by talking about death, he might just be evoking the spirit of death upon himself. He forgot that death is powerless because Jesus is in control, having personally unlocked death's prison. He forgot that the power of life and death reside with the Father.

Does talking about money make anyone wealthy without their lifting a finger? Of course not! The same logic applies to talking about death. The following quotable quote reflects the attitude of some Christians today: *"Everybody wants to go to Heaven, but nobody wants to die!"*

Psalm 49 makes an interesting contrast between people whose hope is in Christ and those who are devoid of fellowship with God. While inescapable death is the destiny of the ungodly who have made wealth their god, death fades entirely from the view of those who are in deep fellowship with God.

Christians facing death should let their words contain the assurance of the resurrection. That is why the psalmist confessed, "But God will redeem my life from the grave; he will surely take me to himself" (Psalm 49:15).

The psalmist firmly believed that as he lived in communion with God, nothing could affect that fellowship because death had lost its sting. This is the hope of faith that reaches beyond physical death and, in so doing, overcomes death spiritually.

Job 19:25-27 seems to support the psalmist's argument above, as Job emphasizes that death cannot destroy his fellowship with God. He knows that physical death is not the end of his existence and that one day he will stand in the presence of his faithful Redeemer and see Him face to face. The above revelations probably assisted his decision-making process in Job 3:21 and 7:15, when he had entertained thoughts of suicide. Job did not opt for early departure.

However, Psalm 73 in its entirety really captures our state of mind and true reaction toward the fear of death. The psalmist, having been through hell on earth, battered by circumstances without end, was on the verge of giving up and renouncing his faith as a phase of blindness and foolishness. He was unable to comprehend rationally how ultimately everything works together for the good of those who love the Lord. However, the Lord—who promises never to leave nor forsake us—lived up to His promise, and the psalmist experienced the reality of His presence. The Spirit witnessed to his spirit, "I am with you always, to the very end of the age" (Matthew 28:20).

After the presence of the Lord was manifested, the psalmist began to see things in a new dimension that had previously escaped his perception. And as a result he declared that if God is for him who can be against him? And he received the assurance that communion with God is indestructible.

For the psalmist, the agonizing hours of doubt and mental anguish were replaced with the joy of liberation from perplexity and fear, and he was able to affirm that anyone who has God has life. Although Psalm 73 does not talk specifically about glorification, the psalmist certainly expected the continuation of his communion with God in the life after the resurrection. This, to him, could not be interrupted by death.

Whenever we entertain the fear of death, we need to remember the words of the prophet Isaiah, who said, "On this mountain he will destroy the shroud that enfolds all peoples, the sheet that covers all nations; he will swallow up death forever. The Sovereign LORD will wipe away the tears from all faces; he will remove the disgrace of his people from all the earth. The LORD has spoken" (Isaiah 25:7-8).

This is a word of reassurance and a promise to take away the veil that has kept us in spiritual blindness and ignorance. Jesus has fulfilled that in His finished work on the Cross and has brought us light, through the gospel, which dispels darkness. People whose hope is not rooted in Jesus may be temporarily happy because of their wealth or earthly bliss, and so for them to die is a wretched thing. However, Christians need to rejoice because "weeping may endure for a night, but joy comes in the morning" (Psalm 30:5). Our new location assures us of eternity with our Maker.

Isaiah continues the same consolation in Isaiah 26:19 by assuring us believers that the dead among us will be raised up. He then encourages the living to bring our thoughts and struggles to the Lord as only He can protect us. We need to recognize that through Him we are the source of life to this dying world.

Furthermore, we see the first clear reference to the resurrection of both the righteous and the wicked in Daniel 12:2, where the prophet says, "Multitudes who sleep in the dust of the earth will awake: some to everlasting life, others to shame and everlasting contempt."

Jesus also assures believers that faith and life are connected when He says that the person whose faith is in Him has already crossed over from death to eternal life (John 5:24). The second death has no power over the believer (Revelation 2:11; 20:6). He is free from the law of sin and death (Romans 8:2).

Since we are fully convinced that Jesus suffered death for everyone and that He is alive forevermore; like Lazarus, our loved ones who are sleeping in the Lord will be awakened. Jesus said, "Our friend Lazarus is at rest and sleeping; but I am going there that I may awaken him out of his sleep" (John 11:11, Amplified Version). Jesus fulfilled His promise, as we then read, "And out walked the man who had been dead, his hands and feet wrapped in burial cloths (linen strips), and with a (burial) napkin bound around his face" (John 11:44, Amplified Version).

Jesus' finished work on the Cross has already freed our loved ones from their burial wrappings because He won the battle against death 2,000 years ago.

The good news is that God has surrendered His only beloved Son to the Cross, thereby depriving death of its power, in order to destroy life and separate the faithful from God. Through the raising of Christ from the dead, fellowship with God in the midst of suffering and death is made available to all those who accept Christ and believe (Romans 10:9). The power that raises Jesus from the dead is still available to us believers. Our Lord is not a God of the dead but of the living, as Matthew 22:31-32 declares: "But about the resurrection of the dead—have you not read what God said to you, 'I am the God of Abraham, the God of Isaac, and the God of Jacob'? He is not the God of the dead but of the living."

Let us all be assured that death does not signify the end because of Christ's finished work. In the death and resurrection of Christ, the hope expressed in Isaiah 25:8 that death would be swallowed up in victory, has been realized. And in the resurrection of our Lord, we have the assurance of our own resurrection (John 11:25-26).

Roger Carswel, in his little book *Comfort in Times of Sorrow*, tells the story of a Scottish Covenanter who spoke the following words before being executed on July 27. 1681: "The Lord knows, I go up this ladder in less fear and perturbed of mind than ever I entered the pulpit to preach—Farewell, all relations and friends in Christ; farewell all acquaintances and earthly enjoyments; farewell reading and preaching, praying and believing, wanderings, reproaches and sufferings. Welcome joy unspeakable and full of glory. Welcome Father, Son, and Holy Ghost. Into thy hands I commit my spirit."

What a great confidence that Coventer must have had in the Lord! I am fully persuaded that he was not disappointed. It is my prayer that we would all learn something from the words of this man who was completely sold out for Christ.

Isaiah 57:1-2 says, "The righteous perish, and no one ponders it in his heart; devout men are taken away, and no one understands that the righteous are taken away to be spared from evil. Those who walk uprightly enter into peace; they find rest as they lie in death."

The prophet describes the condition of believers in death. While the wicked see death as ruin and there is no peace for them, the righteous are assured of peace in their death. Another example of this may be found in 2 Kings 22:19-20, where the righteous King Josiah was assured that he would die before disaster struck. Josiah was assured that the final judgment on Judah and Jerusalem would not come in his days. In like manner, some of us believers may die early because the Lord wants to spare us from impending disasters.

SOME ANTIDOTES TO THE FEAR OF DEATH

In times past more people seemed to believe in God unquestioningly. People believed in life after death, which was a source of comfort and relief to the dying. Christians believe in a reward in Heaven for people who have suffered on earth, depending on the courage, grace, and degree to which they honored God in their lifetime. But such a belief has long since died for many people.

This change is rapidly leading people to live in a state of selfishness and cruelty because they do not believe in eternal judgment nor in eternal life. If there is no reward in Heaven, suffering becomes purposeless. It is the purpose of the Church to give hope to the hopeless and call humanity into a right relationship with God, our Creator. He loves us so much that He willingly gave His only Son as sacrifice for our sin. "But He was wounded for our transgressions, He was bruised for our guilt and iniquities; the chastisement (needful to obtain) peace and well-being for us was upon Him, and with the stripes (that wounded) Him we are healed and made whole" (Isaiah 53:5, Amplified Version).

THE COMMON VIEW

Some believe the Church has lost the original purpose for her existence. That Church today is all about socializing, dancing, networking, and preaching the prosperity gospel rather than giving hope and preaching the full gospel of our Lord Jesus Christ. If that is true, then the Church has become irrelevant in the lives of people, which is a tragedy as we may not be helping to understand the meaning of life and the giving of hope to the hopeless. Notwithstanding that some churches appear lukewarm and devoid of the power of the Holy Spirit, I must put on record that I believe the Church is still relevant today and working harder than ever before to restore broken relationships with God.

Society has contributed to our denial of life after death through unbelief in the finished work of Christ. This has given us neither hope nor purpose; instead it has only increased our anxiety and contributed to our destructiveness and aggression toward one another in an attempt to avoid the reality of our immortality.

In summary, the fear of death is a universal fear. Whether we believe in life after death or not, there is still real loss, pain, and grief when someone dies. The dying person still goes through the reaction phases described earlier in this chapter. It is all right to grieve and mourn briefly for the loss of people and things that we held dear; but when we grieve, we should remember the unconditional love of Christ for us that enabled Him to endure the painful torture of the Cross.

The world has coined new expressions for death, such as *passed away* or *departed; fallen asleep,* and *passed on to glory.* While these may have taken the sting out of death, they do not remove the fact that the person exists no more in an earthly form. The knowledge that our loved ones are with Jesus should be comforting. That is the only thing that can really take the sting out of the pain of a death.

To the non-Christian, death is a tragedy because for him it is the end of his labor, aspiration, desire, and lifetime ambition. The mansions, wealth, cars, friends, and families cannot be taken with him. There is nothing to look forward to except for discovering the realities of eternal punishment. However, it is not all doom and gloom because, if you are reading this book right now, you still have a second chance to begin a new life in Christ Jesus. Those who are in Heaven are not there through works of righteousness but because they have renounced their old sinful ways and invited Jesus into their lives. You, too, can invite Jesus into your life today, no matter what terrible things you may have done. He died for sinners and cares about your soul. He is a lifesaver and not a destroyer.

If you would like Jesus to save you from the stronghold of death, please go to Appendix 1 of this book to make a personal confession of your own sin and ask Him to come into your life and be your Lord. In order to endure life, you need to prepare yourself for death by aligning your spirit with the one who has power over death—Jesus. You need to recognize that death was not part of the original plan of Creation; it is, rather, a by-product of sin. It is also important to note that in order to fully live in this life, we must resolve the problem of death through salvation into eternal life.

Move from Death to Life

Christians need not fear the isolation of death, for we believe in the glorification that comes to us at death and afterwards; and we know that nothing can separate us from God (Romans 8:38-39). It is important to realize that this attitude is not a denial of death but a recognition of the sovereignty of the covenant of God, despite the real loss that is caused by death. We need to show the world how Jesus conquered death on the Cross, how the love of the Father has removed the sting from death, and how we now view death (or Christ's return) with joy and a healthy expectation (Philippians 1:20).

We need to remember and affirm the saying of Jesus: "I am the resurrection and the life. He who believes in me will live, even though he dies"(John 11:25).

When we recognize that physical death is not the end of life, but rather the door to eternal life for those who believe in Jesus Christ, we can say with D.L. Moody, "Earth recedes, Heaven opens before me! If this is death, it is sweet." However, we should be willing to declare that, "If we live, we live to the Lord; and if we die, we die to the Lord. So, whether we live or die, we belong to the Lord" (Romans 14:8).

If our spirits can catch this revelation, the fear of death and its sting will be disarmed. Paul assures us in 1 Corinthians 15:42-44 that God will take a perishable, weak, sinful body and in the resurrection make it imperishable, glorious, and powerful—fit to live eternally with God.

Let us celebrate life and thank God as Isaiah does, "For Sheol (the place of the dead) cannot confess and reach out the hand to You, death cannot praise and rejoice in You; they who go down to the pit cannot hope for your faithfulness (to Your promises; their probation is at an end, their destiny is sealed). The living, the living—they shall thank and praise You, as I do this day; the father shall make known to the children Your faithfulness and Your truth" (Isaiah 38:18-19, Amplified Version).

Sons of the living Jesus, let us tell those around us about the saving grace of Jesus and transmit the name of God to posterity. Praise Him, know Him, and have a meaningful relationship with Him, for the dead cannot sing His praise. Death cannot separate us from God, and the death of Jesus means victory for all His followers. Christ is the Author of life and the Lord both of the dead and the living (Romans 14:9).

At this stage, I would like to conclude this chapter with Paul's prayer for the believers of Ephesus, so that we may experience the power of the resurrection on a daily basis: "And (so that you can know and understand) what is the immeasurable and unlimited and surpassing greatness of His power in and for us who believe, as demonstrated in the working of His mighty strength, which He exerted in Christ when He raised Him from the dead and seated Him at His (own) right hand in heavenly (places), far above all rule and authority and power and dominion" (Ephesians 1:19-21, Amplified Version).

LIGHT RELIEF TO A RATHER CONSUMING TOPIC

How Suggestion Killed a Man[3]

Like the fear of failure, people who have an unhealthy fear of death sometimes invite an untimely death through an inordinate level of worry. In his book, *The Power of Your Subconscious Mind,* Joseph Murphy told a story of how suggestion killed a man.

A crystal-gazer in India told a man that he would die at the next new moon. This man, who was healthy and full of life before the event, called everyone in his family to tell them about the prediction.

He met with his lawyers to update his will and became withdrawn and an invalid as the predicted date drew nearer. On the predicted date, he suffered a fatal heart attack. He died not knowing he was the cause of his own death. It was by his own fear and expectation of the end, accepted as true by his subconscious mind, that he brought about his death.

A person who has conceded defeat in a boxing match or hundred-meter race cannot win that race except by divine intervention. It will not happen unless God wants to teach us a lesson that, in spite of our poor self-image, He is still on the throne and can do anything for us even if we are filled with unbelief. I remember, during the reign of Mike Tyson as the undisputed world heavyweight boxing champion, that some of his opponents seemed to have lost the fight before climbing into the ring with him. The battle had been lost in their minds because they had watched him mercilessly beat other opponents into submission. Their faith was saying, "It is not possible". Ironically, the day Mike Tyson lost the coveted title you could tell by watching his body language that, though his body was present, his mind was elsewhere. The battle had already been lost in his mind. It is important for man to defend himself psychologically against the fear of death or defeat.

If we are really sick and near the point of death and have already accepted the situation, it is unlikely that we will survive. Conversely, there are many stories of people of faith who have fought cancer and won with an unquenchable faith in the Lord—the result was total healing. We need to balance this statement with the recognition that, irrespective of our strong faith in the healing power of Jesus, we are all subject to the timing of our Creator. When He says it's time to come home, nothing we do or don't do can stop Him.

Comfort in Times of Sorrow[4]

A sailing ship spreads her white sails to the morning breeze as she sets sail for the ocean. She looks beautiful and strong. You watch the ship until it seems like a speck of white cloud just where the sea and sky meet each other. Someone next to you says, "There, she's gone."

But has she gone? She is just as large in mast and hull as she was when she left the shore. Just at the moment when someone says, "She's gone," another voice on a distant shore shouts, "She's here!"

Death is similar. Earth's loss is eternity's gain. Death opens the door to the glory of Heaven, where we will be with the Lord and our departed ones forever. Each one of us has an endless existence, first in this world and then in the next. May you be comforted in your grief by these words of encouragement.

BIBLE VERSES TO HELP US

1. "I will ransom them from the power of the grave; I will redeem them from death. Where, O death, are your plagues? Where, O grave, is your destruction" (Hosea 13:14)?
2. "Therefore, just as sin entered the world through one man, and death through sin, and in this way death came to all men, because all sinned" (Romans 5:12).
3. "For the wages of sin is death, but the gift of God is eternal life in Christ Jesus our Lord" (Romans 6:23).
4. "For God so loved the world that he gave his one and only son, that whoever believes in him shall not perish but have eternal life" (John 3:16).
5. "Now listen, you who say, 'Today or tomorrow we will go to this or that city, spend a year there, carry on business and make money.' Why, you do not even know what will happen tomorrow. What is your life? You are a mist that appears for a little while and then vanishes. Instead, you ought to say, 'If it is the Lord's will, we will live and do this or that'" (James 4:13-15).
6. "Just as man is destined to die once, and after that to face judgment, so Christ was sacrificed once to take away the sins of many people; and he will appear the second time, not to bear sin, but to bring salvation to those who are waiting for him." (Hebrews 9:27-28)
7. "But God will redeem my life from the grave; he will surely take me to himself" (Psalm 49:15).
8. "On this mountain he will destroy the shroud that enfolds all peoples, the sheet that covers all nations; he will swallow up death

forever. The Sovereign LORD will wipe away the tears from all faces; he will remove the disgrace of his people from all the earth. The LORD has spoken" (Isaiah 25:7-8).

9. "I am the resurrection, and the life: he that believeth in me, though he were dead, yet shall he live: And whosoever liveth and believeth in me shall never die. Believest thou this" (John 11:25-26, KJV)?

10. "Whether we live, we live unto the Lord; and whether we die, we die unto the Lord; whether we live therefore, or die, we are the Lord's" (Romans 14:8, KJV).

11. "We believe that Jesus died and rose again and so we believe that God will bring with Jesus those who have fallen asleep in him" (1 Thessalonians 4:14).

12. "But that the dead are raised (from death)—even Moses made known and showed in the passage concerning the (burning) bush, where he calls the Lord, The God of Abraham, the God of Isaac, and the God of Jacob. Now He is not the God of the dead, but of the living, for to Him all men are alive (whether in the body or out of it) and they are alive (not dead) unto Him (in definite relationship to Him)" (Luke 20:37-38, Amplified Version).

13. "And God shall wipe away all tears from their eyes; and there shall be no more death, neither sorrow, nor crying, neither shall there be any more pain: for the former things are passed away" (Revelation 21:4, KJV).

14. "Since the children have flesh and blood, he too shared in their humanity so that by His death He might destroy him who holds the power of death—that is, the devil—and free those who all their lives were held in slavery by their fear of death" (Hebrews 2:14-15).

15. "This is in keeping with my own eager desire and persistent expectation and hope, that I shall not disgrace myself nor be put to shame in anything; but that with the utmost freedom of speech and unfailing courage, now as always heretofore, Christ (the Messiah) will be magnified and get glory and praise in this body of mine and be boldly exalted in my person, whether through (by) life or through (by) death" (Philippians 1:20, Amplified Version)

16. "I am (Myself) the Resurrection and the Life. Whoever believes in (adheres to, trusts in, and relies on) Me, although he may die, yet

he shall live; And whoever continues to live and believes in (has faith in, cleaves to, and relies on) Me shall never (actually) die at all. Do you believe this" (John 11:25-26, Amplified Version)?

17. "The righteous perish, and no one ponders it in his heart; devout men are taken away, and no-one understands that the righteous are taken away to be spared from evil. Those who walk uprightly enter into peace; they find rest as they lie in death" (Isaiah 57:1-2).

18. "But we see Jesus, who was made a little lower than the angels, now crowned with glory and honor because he suffered death, so that by the grace of God he might taste death for everyone" (Hebrews 2:9).

19. "I tell you the truth, if anyone keeps my word, he will never see death" (John 8:51).

20. "For Christ's love compels us, because we are convinced that one died for all, and therefore all died. And he died for all, that those who live should no longer live for themselves but for him who died for them and was raised again" (2 Corinthians 5:14-15).

21. "Brothers, we do not want you to be ignorant about those who fall asleep, or to grieve like the rest of men, who have no hope" (1 Thessalonians 4:13).

Finally, you may want to declare, as Paul did claiming the promise of redemption from death: "Where, O death, is your victory? Where, O death, is your sting" (1 Corinthians 15:55)?

END NOTES

1. Evans, Philip. *The Family Medical Reference Book*. Little, Brown and Company (UK), Ltd, 2001.
2. Wakely, Robin. In his sermon "From Fear to Hope" (1986).
3. Murphy, Joseph. *The Power of Your Subconscious Mind*. Pocket Books, 2000.
4. Carswell, Roger. "Comfort in Times of Sorrow."

SIX

FEAR OF CHANGE

We are told that change is an inevitable part of life and are constantly bombarded with various change strategies at work, church, and within our circle of friends. Our parents never stopped preaching the concept of change, and the lifetime-evangelist never gives up hope that one day all of us will live in Christ. While most of us believe that we need change in some area of our lives, others find it difficult to embrace the process of change. Yet the most astute people say, "Before things change, first I must change."

The main purpose of this chapter is to investigate the process of change, expose the reason why people are afraid to embrace change, and encourage readers to actively pursue change because it is an inevitable part of life. God is the only unchangeable one. He is the one who loves us unconditionally, irrespective of our past, present, and future. He is always calling us to change. When we are yet sinners and living daily in sin, He calls us to himself. The process of salvation is all about change from the kingdom of darkness to that of light, from death to life, and from separation to communion. He calls us to renew our minds daily and put on the nature of Christ. *This is the call to change.*

The interesting thing is that changes happen to us all the time, whether they are voluntary or enforced. In order to move from infancy to adulthood, we need to change the way we do things, the way we talk, the way we relate to others, and the food we eat. Learning requires change, as those study methods that have served us faithfully in the past may not be adequate today.

The working environment has changed in its use of various work patterns, from part-time, to home working, consulting staff, agency staff, and fixed-term contracts. The advent of computers has revolutionized the way we work and live and even the way we worship. Computers are no longer considered an invention of the devil and are now an integral part of church administration, communication, and outreach to the wider world.

The world is changing. The United Kingdom, which had been responsible for spreading the good news to most African countries, is now on the receiving end of evangelism from African missionaries. The Soviet Union has collapsed, and along with it has come the collapse of religious persecution from the highest level, and people from these states are now open to the good news of the gospel of Jesus Christ. Europe has regressed from being one of the promoters of the Christian faith to being a persecutor of Christianity and a promoter of Islam and every sinful way in a bid to be politically correct.

The Muslims in the Middle East region fight hard to defend their religion. Despite the use of suicide bombers to eliminate those who oppose them, the fact remains that they are slowly opening up their frontiers to the good news of Jesus Christ. Asia and South America are fast becoming a fertile land for evangelists and missionaries.

Americans are at the forefront of almost everything—the good, the bad, and the ugly. America has become the modern Israel—God's own country, because they are currently taking the name of Jesus to a higher level. They have made resources available for teaching, correcting, evangelizing, and training men and women of God in the way of righteousness so that they may be fully equipped.

After reading all the above, can anyone say that change does not take place in the world? The good news is that God meets with His people in the midst of all life's changes.

Change Drivers

Without wanting to be a prophet of doom, I believe that today is just a warm-up for a more complex world where everything will operate at a much faster rate of change due to the numerous change drivers. The first of these change drivers is people; we are really multiplying and replenishing the earth, and our population is growing very fast.

People cause change as they create things, come up with new ideas, and compete for scarce resources.

The second change driver is technology. As technology is the product of the human race, we can expect the rate of technological change to grow rapidly as people come up with new ways to do things.

The third powerful driver is information. There is an insatiable quest for knowledge today, and word has it that the amount of information available in the world is doubling every five years. With all the knowledge acquired, and with the advancement in technology, information is becoming readily available to more people than it has ever reached before. The pressure to stay at the top and to be better informed will surely increase the stress level to the point where a series of changes in career as well as the way we work is inevitable. Learning how to identify, handle, and embrace change will become a much sought-after skill, and our actions today should go a long way to reducing our level of stress tomorrow.

If changes are an inevitable part of life, why do we generally find it difficult to make them? Most of us probably know people who regularly talk about giving up smoking, drinking, or an immoral lifestyle; of changing career; or living in the life of Christ and doing God's will. Yet they start, only to give up along the way. Some do not even start; their idea remains just that—a good idea or a plan, a bit like a New Year's resolution that loses its appeal on the first day or by the end of January. Why, I ask? Why can't we keep our promises? Is it because of laziness, or are we simply terrified of making those changes?

A CALL FOR CHRIST-CENTERD CHANGE

Some are forever putting off making a life-changing decision to follow Jesus, while others are forever answering the altar call only to backslide the very next day. They step out when the Word of God is powerfully preached and they are under the Holy Spirit's conviction, but then they kill off the fire when the effect of their decision dawns upon them. The thought of attending church services, learning God's Word, and turning their backs on the old ways fills their hearts with fright. They worry about their partners in sin, and they are controlled by people's opinions. What would their friends and families say once they start living out their new faith? Or what if peripheral friends would start to disappear because light and darkness cannot co-habit?

Some of us are already walking in line with God's will but are resisting His call to move onto higher ground; to stand up in our workplace, and be recognized as Christians who diligently follow the teachings of Christ. The thought of being seen as a freak fills our minds to the extent that we waste perfect opportunities to minister life to someone who passes us by. We have failed to acknowledge Him in the presence of others because of our fear and our need to belong. We have forgotten that our mandate on this earth is to infiltrate the unbelievers and bring His light to the world around us.

The interesting thing is that non-Christians can easily recognize us anyway. There is no place to hide as we are already carrying the mark of Christ by virtue of the Holy Spirit living in us. Instead of hiding the light that cannot be quenched, why not ask Jesus to teach us how to be effective witnesses for Him? We need to come out of the closet and let the Master teach us the secret of life-transforming change.

In line with the Father's will, Jesus Christ had to change His career when He reached the age of thirty. I believe that Jesus had have been an accomplished carpenter for many years, probably operating at the top of His business. I believe He would have had the ability to build furniture that could stand the test of time and would have been adept at customer service. He must have learned how to liaise with customers at all levels. Judging by the way He dealt with the Pharisees and the woman caught in adultery, He must have been accustomed to changing His witnessing or counseling style in order to be effective. All these attributes would have become an invaluable tool for Him when He changed His career to become an agent of change to the world at large.

Whether as a carpenter or a minister of the Word, Jesus would always have done the Father's will. He never tampered with people's free will; He never prayed witchcraft prayers nor condemned people in order to make them feel worthless. Instead, He always built people up. He accepts people as they are (including their built-in talents). However, He also promises to make them better. That is why He told Simon and his brothers, "I will make you fishers of men" (Matthew 4:19).

Jesus desires every individual to use his/her talents to enhance the Kingdom of Heaven. He loves us so much that He desires to empower us to do greater things for the Father. Hallelujah!

Jesus also recognizes peoples' differences, their preferred methods of operation, and their different communication styles, family backgrounds, skills, and personalities. All these differences were not changed in the first disciples but put together in new ways so they could be used according to their area of gifting. They became new men in the Spirit, new creations in Christ Jesus, as Jesus encouraged and empowered them to start operating to their maximum potential.

Jesus always has been interested in the inward changes, the spiritual transformation, in doing God's will as opposed to our own will. He knew that if changes occurred from the inside, outward changes would follow naturally. This happens because a person has made a conscious decision to be transformed from their old ways to follow God's new ways. Inner change becomes apparent as these new ways are gradually acted out.

OUR RESPONSE TO CHANGE

The word *change* is used frequently in our daily vocabulary and everyday activities. When driving, we talk about changing gear downward or upward. We speak of goods changing hands, meaning goods passing from one owner to another. We change clothes, whether into a second outfit or to buy a different design. At times we talk about change of heart, change of life, changing one's mind, changing one's attitude—and the list goes on.

According to *The New Collins Thesaurus* by William T. McLeod[1], to change is to alter, convert, diversify, fluctuate, moderate, modify, reform, re-model, reorganize, restyle, shift, transform, vary, alternate, remove, replace, substitute, swap, or make alteration. A critical look at the above definition reveals that when we change, we actually exchange one thing for another. This could take the form of a new occupation or fresh outlook on life or on the world around us. The process could involve deep soul searching that might lead to a total change of heart or a complete change of attitude. We also speak of change in terms of taking off clothes and putting on different ones, or exchanging money for the same amount in another denomination. All this tells us that change comes in different forms or shapes.

The biblical messages are centerd on effecting lasting changes in one's life. When we change from the ways of the world and make a decision to follow Christ, we change our allegiance. A change has taken place in our spirits, from darkness to light.

FEAR OF CHANGE

Whether we like it or not, change occurs naturally; but often our response is to be afraid. For Christians, it is comforting to know that God meets us in the midst of these changes. Times of change give us a special opportunity to catch a glimpse of God in unprecedented ways and to grow in intimacy with Him.

Being called away to an intimate knowledge of God can be unnerving. Abram was called to intimacy with God, and in the process he lied, trusted in his own strength, and later received a change of name (Abraham) and a change of fortune. He became the father of nations and was blessed in a unique way. The Israelites discovered that the inward enemies of fear, anxiety, and unbelief could become strongholds that stand in the way of the liberating changes God intended. We are like them in many ways.

Changing can be hard work and requires energy to battle against the multitude of credible oppositions and circumstances that seek to frustrate our journey. We need the help and presence of God as we gradually enter into God's plan and calling for our lives. It is all right to ask in faith for the assurance of God's promises in the midst of these oppositions and conflicts. God is not disappointed with us because of our fears and unbelief; instead He takes them on and empowers us as we give them to Him. He is the only one who knows our future and has our spiritual map in His hand, so He takes us away from our familiar but confining environment into the freedom of a faithful future.

In Exodus 14, Moses is confronted with a series of fear-driven questions by the Israelites at the sight of the approaching Egyptian army. However, Moses assures them of God's sovereign control over all things. He answers the people, "Do not be afraid. Stand firm and you will see the deliverance the LORD will bring you today. The Egyptians you see today you will never see again. The LORD will fight for you; you need only to be still" (Exodus 14:13-14).

This is a reminder to us that it is the Lord who fights our battles, and through Him we are guaranteed victory. Therefore the problem we see today (whatever that may be) is only for a short time. It is a divine instrument designed to usher us into God's presence and to release us into our destiny. He only allows the situation in order to glorify himself in our lives.

We are called to be courageous and to let our confidence be rooted in the Lord. If we do this, He will make a way where there appears to be no way. When the hyenas and lions are gnashing their teeth and rubbing their claws in readiness to deliver the killer blow, we will see the mighty hand of God working on our behalf. Instead of crying in defeat, it will be rewarding if we stretch out our hands in prayer over the situation and allow God to work through our faith.

Like the Israelites, we need to move from a position of fear to that of faith, reverence, and trust in the Lord. That is why Proverbs 1:7 says, "The fear of the LORD is the beginning of knowledge, but fools despise wisdom and discipline."

This is a call for change in the way we react to circumstances, obstacles, and challenges. To fear the Lord is to recognize that He has the master plan, and all other things that cause us anxiety are in His hand. When we are fully persuaded of the sovereignty of the Lord, it's time to let go of the past and reach out to possess our birthright. It's time to release our past successes and/or failures to God so that we may be released into new things.

Whatever reason we may have for not wanting to change, we have to accept that some change is inevitable in life. The only unchanging person is God. God uses different methods and agents to bring us into His Kingdom and to achieve His purposes in our lives. We do not need to fear His changes because His love for us is constant. It *never* changes! It is because of His great love that He desires all men to be saved. God wants all of us to have the opportunity to change our allegiance from that of darkness and bondage to light and freedom.

My Experience with Constant Change

Working in one of my secular jobs, I learned a thing or two about change. During a period of four years, we moved around a great deal depending on the project we were assigned. In fact, the longest time I ever worked with the same team was for six months. We were constantly changing seating positions, location, project teams, floors, and managers. The positive side to all those changes was that we got to interact with people from different backgrounds, cultures, and beliefs. We gained better understanding of a whole spectrum of people and therefore became multi-skilled, especially improving our people-skills.

Naturally, the constant changing of circumstances produces problems. People are filled with anxiety as they encounter uncertainty, strife, culture shock, team friction, personality clashes, disorientation, disorganization, and a sometimes totally chaotic environment. However, while I may not have liked the unsettling working environment at the time and sometimes detested its effect upon my domestic arrangements, I have come into the understanding that God put me in it to train me for a fast moving, ever-changing life in the ministry. In fact, those periods of constant change presented me with unique learning opportunities and training on how to stay focused and avoid being disorientated by the constantly changing environment.

At times, our team went through periods of storming, forming, and norming ;and as we entered into a new dawn of trust, collaboration, and cooperation. Then we were disbanded. It made me want to scream, knowing that I then needed to repeat the same process with my new team. In the same manner, when our personal life and routine are altered through changes in our financial situation, social structures, health, or marital status, we are presented with a special opportunity to see God in a new dimension previously unavailable to us.

However, we can be guaranteed that godly changes do not merely occur for their own sake. There is a divine purpose and destination when He calls us to leave a familiar environment for an unfamiliar one. Abram was called to change to become Abraham—the father of nations. We need to prayerfully obey God as He leads us into our destiny.

AGENTS OF CHANGE

God has put within all of us the power to embrace change. We must begin to see ourselves as learners of new things, leaving behind the old things and embracing new moves of God. The Scriptures declare in Isaiah 43:18-19, "Forget the former things; do not dwell on the past. See, I am doing a new thing! Now it springs up; do you not perceive it? I am making a way in the desert and streams in the wasteland."

Here the prophet declares that all the miracles that God wrought in that first redemption were of little importance compared with the more remarkable miracle that would soon be accomplished. Let us open our eyes and see the new things God is doing, things unheard of and uncommon, which on account of their greatness and excellence will overshadow all other works.

The above passage tells me that in order to change we must first see the change in our inner man (spirit). That is, we must perceive the change and then let it manifest in the physical realm. For example, to become more prosperous we must change our perception; we must think in a different way and stop being contented with just getting by. An element of our life strategy must alter before change takes place in the physical realm. To illustrate, if we are used to thinking that money is the root of all evil, our subconscious strategies say, "Do not make money, otherwise you will be enticed to do evil deeds." This is a counter-productive strategy that prevents us from achieving our goal of becoming prosperous. Instead, we should apply Abraham's strategies of seeing prosperity, first in the spiritual, and then possessing all that our eyes can see (Genesis 13:15).

The extent to which we see is the extent to which we are willing to change.

According to the definitions above, change involves giving up one thing and reaching out for another. This process can be traumatic, as we may be filled with anxiety and fear of the unknown, so we may need to ask the Lord for strength to cope with the difficulties that we face and for the courage to do what needs to be done. People desiring to give up smoking may look for chewing gum, but by doing so they simply replace one addiction with another. The real issue is the feelings associated with smoking and the rise in the level of their uncertainty and insecurity. Such uncertainty may produce resistance to change. With any type of change we have to make a conscious decision to be transformed by the renewing of our minds (Romans 12:2).

Be willing to leave behind the old lifestyle in order to enjoy the inheritance of new life.

Prayer is a very important change-agent. Prayer is communion with God and personal recognition and acceptance of the divine will. This tells us that prayer is the engine that moves us from the position of defeat into the presence of God—a place of certain victory. If we make a personal commitment to pray and seek God in prayer, we are saying to Him that we cannot effect the change in our own strength but we rely instead on Him to fully change us by His Spirit. Those who are led by the Spirit of God are sons of God (Romans 8:14).

As we make a personal commitment to pray and do His will, God will make possible the desired changes in our lives.

Change involves investing time, money, and effort in a particular thing, and it certainly requires our obedience and cooperation with the move of God. As our salvation cost Jesus Christ His life, so also our change comes with a sacrifice. Life is a trade-off, and in accordance with the definitions above it sometimes requires a complete change of attitude—a giving up of personal agendas for God's agenda.

True change is never effortless, so we must be fully committed to the process in order for change to occur.

When Jesus called Simon, John and James in Luke 5:10, He said to them, "Have no fear; from now on you will be catching men!" (Amplified Version).

In other words, "Take a risk and allow me to change your lives." Jesus could see through their external posture and beyond their personal confession but He still chose to work with them. In like manner, He tells us to take a risk and come on a personal journey of change with Him.

When we invest in the Kingdom, our returns are guaranteed from above. Our circumstances during the journey may not appear to have changed, our emotion may fluctuate, but we are guaranteed that the predetermined outcome is blessing and success from the Lord. Like Abram we may be unsure of where we are going, but as we obey Him we will surely receive the blessing of obedience (Genesis 12:1-3).

A call to change from God may require us to take unprecedented risks, but the predetermined outcome is blessing and success.

The Color of Change

The Lord created all things, and we were all made to be different but equal. The Apostle Paul fought bravely for equality with the Gentiles, to the displeasure of his own Jewish people. All who have confessed Christ as Lord and Savior are supposed to be born of the same Spirit. The reality is such that we are forever suspicious of one another. We are afraid to worship with one another because of the artificial class system created by different Christian groups.

We articulate our built-in prejudice in the way we preach, teach, and fellowship with one another. We call unclean what God has sanctified and become angry when we find ourselves on the receiving end of such an accusation. Some of us only see African churches, White churches, Jewish believers, and Asian believers; or else, we see Evangelical, Pentecostal, Baptist, Catholic, Anglican, and Methodist denominations, instead of the house of God or the Body of Christ.

Some of our attitudes are simply a result of our culture, manifesting in spite of our spiritual change from darkness to light. By choice, we have prevented the light from shining into this area of our lives. We cannot attend conferences organized by any denomination except our own (and those in our small elite group). Is it possible that we are afraid of cultural and theological differences or simply that we fear change? Are we too frightened to move beyond our comfort zone and enlarge our area of influence?

I believe the Lord is calling us to repent in this area. It's time to change.

In his letter to the Corinthians, the Apostle Paul recognizes the diversity of different spiritual gifts exercised by God's people and emphasizes that we are members of one Body—the Body of Christ. He puts it this way, "The body is a unit, though it is made up of many parts; and though all its parts are many, they form one body. So it is with Christ. For we were all baptized by one Spirit into one body—

whether Jews or Greeks, slave or free—and we were all given the one Spirit to drink" (1 Corinthians 12:12-13).

Paul emphasizes that in Christ there should be no racial, cultural, or social distinction. God has given all His people the Holy Spirit to dwell in us so that our lives may overflow with the fruit of the Spirit (Galatians 5:22-23). Unity in Christ must transcend ethnic, social, and sexual distinctions, for there is neither Jew nor Greek, slave nor free, male nor female, as we are all one in Christ (Galatians 3:28).

THE RELATIONSHIP BETWEEN FEAR, SEGREGATION, AND CHANGE

The following nuggets from the Scriptures can be used to define the relationship between fear, segregation, and change.

1. Exodus 1:9-10

We are told that a new king (probably Ahmose) who did not know Joseph came to power in Egypt. He became afraid of the Israelites and began a reign of terror and mistreatment. Immediately, we notice the existence of in-built jealousy and outward societal segregation fuelled by fear. This condition of heart made the king embark on a consistent and sustained reign of terror designed to weaken the children of God. The king had seen the writing on the wall, and he feared that change was imminent and that justice would prevail over oppression. Like many repressive regimes, for example Saddam of Iraq, Abacha of Nigeria, and Idi-Amin of Uganda, the king in this text did anything and everything possible to resist God-induced change, but failed miserably.

2. Esther 3-5

Haman, terrified of the growing influence and power of the Jews, made an extravagant plan to wipe them out of existence. Again, we see oppression and hatred for a particular group of people, and the misuse of power. The situation started because one man, Mordecai, refused to bow down to Haman and to other gods. While rejoicing in the change of status for himself, Haman could not handle God-induced change in the life of the Jews. He feared the erosion of his power and authority.

3. John 4:3

We see the Pharisees' prejudice against Jesus because He was baptizing more people than John. This is a classic example of success-aroused opposition. The Pharisees could not handle the popularity of Jesus, and His teaching was rocking their world to its very foundation. Like King Ahmose of Egypt and Haman of Persia, the Pharisees' solution was to eliminate the source of the threat. They refused to embrace change induced directly from above, which was actually designed to set them free from bondage to the Law.

4. John 4:9

This is the story of a Samaritan woman's encounter with Jesus. In Exodus 1:9-10, above, we empathize with the Jews because of the injustice they suffered at the hand of the Egyptians. Ironically, we now see the Jews' prejudice against the so-called unclean Samaritan. The woman was surprised that Jesus spoke with her because Jews feared that by relating with Samaritans they too would become unclean.

The above examples expose the issues in our hearts and the danger of internalized prejudice and low self-esteem (especially of the Samaritan woman). The Samaritan now goes about with a devalued self-worth and a feeling of being unclean, to the extent that she almost misses her day of miracle. She was surprised that Jesus took an interest in her—enough to engage her in conversation. She said, "You are a Jew and I am a Samaritan woman. How can you ask me for a drink?" (John 4:9).

The Jews feared physical contamination, yet ignored the spiritual contamination acquired through the antics of the Pharisees. The Pharisees had told the Samaritans that they were unclean so that this woman had internalized feelings of unworthiness through decades of unacceptable practices. Both sides feared change and both refused to embrace it from the Giver of living water. Instead, they preferred to die in their unregenerate condition.

Equally, many religious leaders have sown the seed of hatred, malice, lies, and religious and spiritual poverty in their children, which has remained to this day, serving as a serious obstacle to receiving the gospel of Jesus Christ. It is my prayer that the veil will be removed from their eyes so that God-induced change may take place.

In the same manner I believe today's Church should work harder to ensure that internalized prejudice does not turn people away from God rather than drawing them to Him. The different Christian groups urgently need to break down the walls of disunity. Taboo-style prejudice must be eradicated before our enemies feed on it and create a situation of divide and conquer. We need more collaboration, fellowship, and unity in the Body of Christ. Divided we fall, but in unity we can rule and become the light of the world. We are one Body, baptized into Christ Jesus (1 Corinthians 12:13).

THE CHRIST-CHANGED LIFE

God made man in His own image and made him perfect. As a result of sin, the perfect man became imperfect and also received personality decline by following the ways of the world. Our mandate, however, is to grow more like Jesus. According to Jay E. Adams[2], God has deposited in each of us a gift that Scripture calls *phusis* (nature). The way one uses *phusis* in responding to life's problems and challenges determines our personality. These response patterns may become deeply etched over a period of time, until they become second nature. Although habit patterns are hard to change, it is not impossible to effect a change in all areas of our lives because the Master of change is resident inside us. The word *sanctification* (hagiasmos in Greek) means holiness, purification, and consecration. When the Holy Spirit completes this process in our lives, He produces a great change of separation from unholiness to divine holiness.

God's Word changes people. It changes our thinking, our decisions, and our behavior. All through the Scriptures change is anticipated and we are renewed daily as we put the Word into practice. The Word of God aims to strengthen the individual through changing our behavioral patterns, bringing them into conformity with the biblical standard. The Holy Spirit is the Spirit of change, and He continuously works in our personality. God, throughout history, has turned Abram into Abraham, Jacob into Israel, Simon into Peter, and Saul into Paul. In all these examples we see life-transforming changes. It is comforting to know that He is still in the business of change.

We can see a very good example of a Christ-changed life in the story of Saul of Tarsus. While he was on his way to Damascus to persecute Christians, Jesus changed him. Through his experience, Paul became a new creation in Christ Jesus. Old things had departed, and new things had arrived (2 Corinthians 5:17). Paul became a man who chased after God. Through fellowship with the Holy Spirit, he received a special insight into the Scriptures. Paul became a teacher of the Word and began to break barriers previously reserved for the elite (the Jews) by passionately tearing down the religious wall that prevented the Gentiles from entering into a life-changing relationship with Christ. Jesus identified Paul to Ananias as, "my chosen instrument to carry my name before the Gentiles and their kings and before the people of Israel" (Acts 9:15).

Paul bore the mark of the Cross through many hardships, trials, and tribulations. He was beaten, battered, and bruised; placed in prison with shackles on his hands; and suffered the frustration of ministering to people who failed to appreciate his message. Yet Paul always had a cheerful heart because of the inextinguishable flame of the resurrection life of Jesus burning inside him (2 Corinthians 4:16-17).

Like Thomas (called Didymus) in John 20:24-27, the world may demand to see the nail marks in our hands before they will believe. In His resurrected body, Jesus had to show Thomas the marks of the Cross: signs that He had been through hell and won the victory. I believe Thomas' life must have changed from the moment he saw Jesus' scars because he suddenly declared, "My Lord and my God!" This was a sign that something had clicked and a change of heart had taken place. The good news is that the power that resurrected Jesus Christ is available to all Christians. When we enter into His finished work, we can access the reward and start living victorious and fulfilling lives.

Christ restructured Peter's life when he was in utter despair after his denial (John 21:15-19). However, a radical change took place in Peter's life, and from then on he began to live up to his name *Rock*. Likewise, it was in a time of great fear and distress that God chose to change Jacob's name to Israel. This change took place at a time when Jacob acknowledged God as the source of all blessing. The Lord in turn acknowledged Jacob as His servant by changing his name. Jacob saw God face to face, and his life was never the same again (Genesis 32:7-31).

God has gifted certain people to meet our needs for specific times in our lives. We have also been given gifts to meet the needs of others. God places us into changing situations to open up new opportunities for us to operate in those anointings. We also need to ask God to make us open to giving and receiving the gifts of the Spirit. When things change, we need to see how we fit in the new situation. Some of us will immediately embrace the changes, while others see periods of change as difficult times that take a great deal of effort and energy. Irrespective of our perception of the change-period, we need to know and be fully persuaded that we are connected with each other and have a contribution to make.

As Christians, we need to follow the divine strategy and obey His directions because His plans for us are good and not evil. We should allow God's Word to change our thinking, decisions and behavior. The Lord is the only unchanging one, and His promises concerning us have not changed. In fact they are new every day.

The concept of change should be a thrilling experience rather than a threatening one. Our life is an adventure into God's newness and this need not make us insecure because we fear the unknown. We have not experienced this wonderful future yet, but it is not unknown to God whose plans for us are good. Growth means changing into the fullness of the stature of Christ.

A Story of Positive Change: The Little Me and the Big Me

I have read about the story of Enrico Caruso, the great operatic tenor who was struck with stage fright. The *Little Enrico* wanted to strangle the *Big Enrico* by using the spirit of fear. Spasms caused by intense fear constricted the muscles of his throat. His vocal cords felt paralyzed and useless. Enrico stood backstage, already in costume, while perspiration poured down his face. He was scheduled to go out on the stage and sing before an eager audience of thousands. Trembling, he said, "I can't sing. They will laugh at me. My career is finished."

As he turned to go back to his dressing room, something suddenly changed inside him. He stopped and shouted, "The little me is trying to strangle the Big Me within!"

He turned toward the stage again and stood taller, "Get out of here!" Enrico commanded, addressing the little me. "The Big Me wants to sing through me!" By the Big Me, Enrico meant the limitless power and wisdom of his subconscious mind. He began to shout, "Get out! Get out! The Big Me is going to sing!"

The story concluded that Enrico walked out on stage and sang gloriously and majestically.

There is a saying: *"If you want to change external conditions, you must change the cause."*

Earlier in this chapter I mentioned that in order to change we must see the change first in our inner man (spirit). That is, we must perceive the change and then let it manifest in the physical realm. Most people want to change their conditions and circumstances by working on them with a view to neutralizing their weaknesses. This is not a bad thing; but to neutralize something is temporary and to eliminate it is permanent. We must go right to the heart of an issue, see that the conditions flow from a root cause, and apply the medicine of the Word. To neutralize may just be a terrible waste of time and effort.

Enrico, realizing that destiny calls and stage fright is just another attempt by the enemy of progress to put him inside the box of limitation, decided to speak to his inner mind and deal with the root cause of his problem. That root of the problem was the way Enrico used his subconscious mind. When Enrico challenged the cause of the problem, he changed the effect and entered fully into his calling. I do not know if Enrico was a Christian and do not wish to make assumptions about how he got the revelation that the little Enrico wanted to strangle the Big Enrico. I believe, however, that we can all learn something from Enrico, as we are bound to find ourselves in similar scenarios where the *little us* is working hard to strangle and pervert the call of God in our lives. We need to speak to the little ones, commanding them to make space for the big ones in the name of Jesus. And finally we need to walk out on stage and just do whatever it is because, when we challenge the enemies of progress in our lives, our God is excited and waiting to walk with us in His might and power.

HEAVENLY PROSPECTS

Like insurance salesmen, we often tell people what to do and hit them over the head with our doctrine—in this case the Bible and legalism—without listening to their point of view or learning about their needs. We would be better to simply ask questions and, based on the answers given, meet people at their point of need.

When the needs of the unsaved are met through our prayers or our witness, they will usually then see Jesus in us. The Holy Spirit is then enabled to create a desire in their hearts and, through the conviction of their hearts, removes the remaining barriers to receiving the Word of God. By listening to people and following the direction of the Holy Spirit, we set in motion a chain reaction through which God is empowered to work. He is the only one who can by His Spirit renew, regenerate, and revitalize lives.

Just like insurance salesmen, our prospects are everywhere irrespective of missed opportunities. The next souls are out there waiting to be saved and waiting for the likes of you and me to be the catalyst of change in their lives. Sometimes, however, due to our eagerness to close a sale, we fail to use wisdom in our evangelism and thereby lose the opportunity presented by the Lord for us to partner with Him in depopulating hell.

Who says we have no prospects? The field is all around us and in our neighborhood. The unsaved are walking past our homes, sitting opposite us at work, even living in our own families and crying out for our help. All we have to do is yield to the Holy Spirit's gentle prompting. In John 4:35 Jesus puts it like this, "I tell you, open your eyes and look at the fields! They are ripe for harvest."

Let us accept the charge today to be faithful ambassadors and proclaim the good news wherever He leads.

In the midst of this ever-changing world, I say to you emphatically, *"There is someone who never changes—Jesus. Our Lord is the unchanging one. He is the same yesterday, today, and forever."* He has always been in the business of regenerating and renewing souls. He assures us in Malachi 3:6, "I the LORD do not change." His unchanging presence in a bewildering succession of circumstances is reassuring.

Life may rob us in a moment of every familiar source of support and all our sustaining power. We may look for a fixed point—anything resembling what once sustained us—but find nothing. We look in vain until it dawns upon us that He is still there, still loving, and still protecting us. The closer we are to Him, the safer will be our walk. He does not change!

The Certainty of God's Promise

Hebrews 6:13 reminds us about God's promises to Abraham: "I will surely bless you and make your descendants as numerous as the stars in the sky and the sand on the seashore" (Genesis 22:17). The promise of many descendants was made with an oath—to emphasize its unchanging character.

While man's word is not always trustworthy and at times changes depending on whether you are in a person's good books or not, God's Word is unchanging. You can bank it without the fear of its being returned unpaid. His Word is unchanging, and His oath gives us double confirmation (for those of us who like confirmation!).

The Lord tells Habakkuk to write down the revelation and make it plain on tablets because it's for an appointed time—that even though it tarries, it will surely come to pass (Habakkuk 2:2-3 paraphrased). The Bible also tells us that after waiting patiently for twenty-five years, Abraham received what was promised—the birth of his son Isaac (Genesis 17:2, 18:10, 21:5). This is unwavering faith.

Both our security and our hope are rooted in God's unchanging character. People will make promises one day and disappoint us the next. We can all be fickle and unreliable at times. Circumstances beyond our control may sometimes prevent us from keeping our promises. But God's Word is not yes and no at the same time so that it would be impossible for us to understand what He means. Instead, His Word and His promises are free from ambiguity. They are an affirmative *yes*, and we respond with our unwavering belief, "Amen!" (2 Corinthians 1:17-22).

God's faithfulness and love are not subject to the fluctuations of time nor to human mortality. Unlike man, God does not suffer from fickle whims, irrational mood swings, or inability to handle circumstances.

No amount of change in our lives will affect God's care for us. He is our ever-present help in trouble (Psalm 46:1-2). God's Word gives us the truth that never changes. We find strength and courage when we listen to the voice of God rather than to public opinion. He assures us of the unchanging nature of His character by declaring emphatically, "Heaven and earth will pass away, but my words will never pass away" (Mark 13:31).

Such is my assurance of Him that I dare to declare, "I am the righteousness of Christ," and know that nothing can change that. Hallelujah! I say this not because of anything I have done but because of my trust and confidence in His finished work on the Cross of Calvary. Today God is calling you and me to personal change. Human beings may be described accurately as humans under construction because we are constantly receiving new insight about ourselves and about God. Personalities can be changed. God, throughout history, has turned the Jacobs of this world into Israels, Simons into Peters, and Sauls into Pauls. *Let Him change you!*

Today's personality is based on yesterday's influences. Today's suffering may be the result of yesterday's decisions and compromises. What one describes as today is but a composite of the past. Personality change is the work of the Holy Spirit, as we cannot change ourselves. Ministers of God and other people helpers are just agents whom the Spirit may use to accomplish His work of restoration and sanctification.

THE CALL

If you do not know God or have not confessed Jesus as your personal Savior, today is your chance to change. He says, "Whoever comes to me I will never drive away" (John 6:37).

He has not changed! The assurance is still there for you today just as it was yesterday—especially for those who claim to be too intelligent or sophisticated for such holy stuff.

Are you saying, "I go to church and indeed answered a call like this sometime ago, yet nothing changes"? I say, "Make a renewed commitment to grow in the knowledge of Him. Walk with the Lord like never before." Are you an atheist, agnostic, a Muslim, a Freemason, a

Buddhist, or a Hindu and believe there are many ways to find God? I tell you the strong veil of religion is still masking the truth from you. You can remove it today by moving to the camp of light. He says to you, "No one can see the kingdom of God unless he is born again" (John 3:3).

Are you like Nicodemus (John 3:1 15), a religious leader who was caught up in the religious world? Nicodemus was living in a world of chronic darkness, ignorance, and misinformation, entrenched in the Law of Moses but not born from above by the renewal of the Spirit. He never had asked Jesus to come into his heart.

May I inform you that Moses did not make it to the Promised Land? Therefore, religion cannot save you. Nor can you be saved by trying to be good, by doing the best you can, or by being a member of a social or religious organization. The Word of God says we are not saved by good works (Ephesians 2:8-9).

Do you believe God is useless? Do you ask, "Where is God in my suffering? Is He watching to see when I do wrong things so He can punish me?" I want to assure you that God's eye has been on you ever since you were born, but not so He can criticize you. God has a plan for you—He wants to enjoy a relationship with you. He wants you to be happy. He loves you so much that He willingly gave His one and only Son so that everyone who believes in Him may have eternal life (John 3:16).

We do not have to be perfect for God to care about us. Everyone has messed things up at one time or another. No one can make himself or herself perfect by trying. But God is too great to be stopped by our failures or fears. He says all you have to do is to:

1. Recognize that you cannot save yourself.

2. Acknowledge your sin (Romans 3:10-12) and know that your sins have separated you from God (Isaiah 59:2).

3. Repent and turn from sin to God.

4. Believe that Jesus died for and settled your debt of sin by His death on the Cross of Calvary (Romans 5:8).

5. Believe that He was raised from the dead (Romans 4:25) and now lives to save all those who will come to Him by faith (Hebrews 7:25).

Through prayer, you need to call on the name of the Lord Jesus Christ with a sincere desire to be saved from your sins. Invite Him to become your Lord and personal Savior. He has promised, "Everyone who calls on the name of the Lord will be saved" (Romans 10:13).

If you would like to begin new life in Christ Jesus, a template of a salvation prayer is available in Appendix 1 at the end of this book.

Having confessed Jesus as your Lord and Savior, you need to tell someone as a witness to the fact, find a Bible-believing church where you can have fellowship with other believers, and regularly read the Word of God. Irrespective of whatever circumstances life throws your way, He has promised that no one can take His children out of His hand (John 10:28). His presence surrounds you whether you are aware of it or not; the bond between you and the Lord cannot be broken.

He assures us that in our journey with change, "My Presence will go with you, and I will give you rest" (Exodus 33:14).

God does not change. His promises and assurance are forever. Any promises made to us will surely come to pass in due time and season.

Pray this Prayer: Lord, change me so that I may be a perfect reflection of Your will and purpose for my life. I need more of You in my life. Change my life, my thought processes, and my character so that I may fully access Your finished work on the Cross and live a holy life that brings You glory.

Remember, God's Word changes people, changes our thinking, our decisions, and our behavior. Though habit patterns are hard to change, such change is not impossible. The Scriptures everywhere anticipate change. The Holy Spirit is the Spirit of change. But *one thing* never changes—His promises. And *someone* never changes—the Lord. His Word gives us the truth that never changes. He is the same yesterday, today, and forever.

[Note: *If you have received Jesus as your Lord and Savior in the above calls to salvation, please share your story with us. Send your testimony to*: admin@thefearfactorbooks.com or post it on the author's website http://www.thefearfactorbooks.com]

ANTIDOTES TO THE FEAR OF CHANGE

Change is the only thing in life that is 100-percent guaranteed to happen (except that one day we will die). Change is an inevitable part of life and occurs over time. At times it doesn't need our permission—for example the process of physical growth from baby to adult is automatic and does not need our approval.

All who who live on planet earth have things in their lives they would like to change. It could be an attitude, a perspective, or an outlook on life. At times we get things so wrong that we think it is not worth trying to change and make amends. Perhaps we have sinned against people and God, and we are guilt-stricken, or our pride prevents us from apologizing and confessing our sins to God. So we cannot move on. Or perhaps we think we are not making any progress in the Christian life; that God will not forgive us if we repeat the same old sins continuously. This is a lie from the pit of hell because the Lord never gets tired of the Prodigal Son returning home. There are heavenly parties whenever a prodigal returns!

My mandate is to encourage everyone in this predicament that guilt or pride only denies us from accessing God's plan for our lives. The Bible tells us, "If we confess our sins, he is faithful and just and will forgive us our sins and purify us from all unrighteousness" (1 John 1:9).

This is a call to change our reaction when we fall short of God's Word. We need to snap out of the guilt trip, forgive ourselves, and confess our struggles to God, who is able to forgive us and make us right with Him. The above process is equally useful for restoring one another when we sin against each other.

It is important that we meet with God when we are in the midst of life-changing circumstances. A change of attitude is required when we find ourselves on a tightrope, where nothing seems to work and no one appears to care for us. We need to undertake an attitude audit and eliminate traits that have become a hindrance to us by asking God to help us change.

Our attitude should be to turn toward God because the solution to our problems can only be found in Him. Turning to God could entail one or more of the disciplines below:

1. Searching for the Word of God regarding our situation
2. Looking at ourselves in the light of His Word
3. Confessing our faults and anything else that is revealed to us by the Holy Spirit
4. Obeying God's Word as the Scriptures say, "We know that we have come to know him if we obey his commands" (1 John 2:3).
5. Staying in the place of prayer, as prayer is the engine that takes us into the presence of God—a place of life-transforming change.
6. Thanking God for answering our prayers and being prepared for God-induced change without putting God in a box—that is, to expect God to change you using specific methods. His ways are not ours, and His plans for us are usually too superior for our finite minds to comprehend (Isaiah 55:8-9).

It has been said that, "attitude affects altitude". It is our attitude toward God and life that makes or breaks us. We need to change our attitudes and mindsets toward many issues in life, as we cannot honestly say we love God if we are not prepared to change and reflect His image.

For those readers struggling with life changes and feeling defeated, I would like to encourage you that this process takes time, commitment, determination, prayer, obedience, and the will to succeed against all odds. It may take days, months, or years, but with God's active involvement change will surely be manifest.

Bible Verses to Help Us

1. "Forget the former things; do not dwell on the past. See, I am doing a new thing! Now it springs up; do you not perceive it? I am making a way in the desert and streams in the wasteland" (Isaiah 43:18-19).
2. "The Lord has sworn and will not change his mind: 'You are a priest forever, in the order of Melchizedek'" (Psalm 110:4 and Hebrews 7:21).
3. "I the LORD do not change" (Malachi 3:6).

4. "Every good and perfect gift is from above, coming down from the Father of the heavenly lights, who does not change like shifting shadows" (James 1:17).

5. "And he said: 'I tell you the truth, unless you change and become like little children, you will never enter the kingdom of heaven'" (Matthew 18:3).

6. "Be transformed by the renewing of your mind" (Romans 12:2).

7. "The angel said to those who were standing before him, 'Take off his filthy clothes.' Then he said to Joshua, 'See, I have taken away your sin, and I will put rich garments on you'" (Zechariah 3:4).

8. "Repent, then, and turn to God, so that your sins may be wiped out, that times of refreshing may come from the Lord" (Acts 3:19).

9. "And we, who with unveiled faces all reflect the Lord's glory, are being transformed into his likeness with ever-increasing glory, which comes from the Lord, who is the Spirit" (2 Corinthians 3:18).

10. "Forgetting what is behind and straining toward what is ahead, I press on toward the goal to win the prize for which God has called me heavenward in Christ Jesus" (Philippians 3:13-14).

11. "But our citizenship is in heaven. And we eagerly await a Savior from there, the Lord Jesus Christ, who, by the power that enables him to bring everything under his control, will transform our lowly bodies so that they will be like his glorious body" (Philippians 3:20-21).

12. "For the Son of God, Christ Jesus (the Messiah), Who has been preached among you by us, by myself, Silvanus, and Timothy, was not Yes and No; but in Him it is (always the divine) Yes. For as many as are the promises of God, they all find their Yes (answer) in Him (Christ). For this reason we also utter the Amen (so be it) to God through Him (in His Person and by His agency) to the glory of God" (2 Corinthians 1:19-20, Amplified Version).

13. "Therefore we were buried with Him through baptism into death, that just as Christ was raised from the dead by the glory of the Father, even so we also should walk in newness of life" (Romans 6:4, NKJV).

14. "But thanks be to God that, though you used to be slaves to sin, you wholeheartedly obeyed the form of teaching to which you were

entrusted. You have been set free from sin and have become slaves to righteousness. I put this in human terms because you are weak in your natural selves, just as you used to offer the parts of your body in slavery to impurity and to ever-increasing wickedness, so now offer them in slavery to righteousness leading to holiness" (Romans 6:17-19).

15. "So Jacob said to his household and to all who were with him, 'Get rid of the foreign gods you have with you, and purify yourselves and change your clothes'" (Genesis 35:2).

16. "After Jacob returned from Paddan Aram, God appeared to him again and blessed him. God said to him, 'Your name is Jacob, but you will no longer be called Jacob; your name will be Israel.' So he named him Israel" (Genesis 35:9-10).

17. "If a man dies, shall he live again? All the days of my hard service I will wait, Till my change comes" (Job 14:14, NKJV).

18. You prevail forever against him, and he passes on; You change his countenance and send him away" (Job 14:20, NKJV).

19. "But He is unique, and who can make Him change? And whatever His soul desires, that He does" (Job 23:13, NKJV).

20. "In whose eyes a vile person is despised, But he honours those who fear the LORD; He who swears to his own hurt and does not change" (Psalm 15:4, NKJV).

21. "God will hear, and afflict them, even He who abides from of old. Selah. Because they do not change, Therefore they do not fear God" (Psalm 55:19, NKJV).

22. "They will perish, but You will endure; Yes, they will all grow old like a garment; Like a cloak You will change them, And they will be changed" (Psalm 102:26, NKJV).

23. "My son, fear the LORD and the king; Do not associate with those given to change" (Proverbs 24:21, NKJV).

24. "Can the Ethiopian change his skin or the leopard its spots? Then may you also do good who are accustomed to do evil" (Jeremiah 13:23, NKJV).

25. "The more they increased, The more they sinned against Me; I will change their glory into shame" (Hosea 4:7, NKJV).

26. "For I am the LORD, I do not change; Therefore you are not consumed, O sons of Jacob" (Malachi 3:6, NKJV).

27. "For we have heard him say that this Jesus of Nazareth will destroy this place and change the customs Moses handed down to us" (Acts 6:14).
28. "For the priesthood being changed, of necessity there is also a change of the law" (Hebrews 7:12, NKJV).

End Notes

1. McLeod, William T. *The New Collins Thesaurus*. Collins, 1984.
2. Adams, Jay E. *Competent to Counsel*. Grand Rapids, Michigan: Zondervan Publishing House 1970.

SEVEN

FROM FEAR TO LOVE

The purpose of this chapter is to encourage readers to move on from using fear as a means of controlling people and instead to relate with one another using the most excellent way—that is, love. In this chapter we are also going to compare the sources and effects of fear and love so that we may be able to spot them quickly when we see both in operation. The Bible tells us, "There is no fear in love. But perfect love drives out fear, because fear has to do with punishment. The one who fears is not perfect in love" (1 John 4:18).

My experience indicates that most people, whether inside or outside the Church, believe that "God is love." We believe that God is kind, understanding, merciful, and loving. Yet some cannot comprehend that God is alive, active, and loving at all. Instead, they see all the suffering, injustice, and cruelty in the world today and ask, "If God is loving, why do we have so much suffering?" Some have been privileged to read the Old Testament and have succinctly summarized it as follows: If you are good and obey the Lord, He will be kind and will prosper you; but if you are disobedient and arouse His wrath, then He will most surely destroy you. They have come to believe in the law of retaliation—an eye for an eye (Exodus 21:24) and cannot see, feel, or enjoy a personal relationship with a God who is just and merciful and yet loving. But Jesus preached that love was more important than respecting the rules. He said that in order to operate in love, we must forget about "eye for eye, and tooth for tooth" (Matthew 5:38).

While some religious leaders today use fear and manipulation (spiritual witchcraft) to hold on to their followers, Jesus came to set His followers free from the bondage of religion and the clutches of death. He did this through His teaching, preaching, acts of love, and

His self-sacrifice on the Cross. He died for us all while we were still sinners. How many people would willingly lay down their lives for the righteous? Probably very few. Jesus did it for all of us. This was unconditional love in action.

Jesus' teaching promotes love and mercy. We see an example of His teachings from the parable of the lost son, popularly known as "The Prodigal Son." In this parable, we read about the young son who wanted to be free of parental restraint and so requested his inheritance. The father agreed to his request and allowed him to seek pastures new. After squandering his inheritance, the wayward son came to his senses and returned home. The action of the father should be an example in the world today. Instead of living a culture of "one-strike and you're out" or "zero tolerance." we should emulate this loving father.

The Bible tells us in Luke 15:20, "But while he was still a long way off, his father saw him and was filled with compassion for him; he ran to his son, threw his arms around him and kissed him."

The story reveals the heart of a loving father who was very happy to see his lost son come back home, and with eyes of love ran to meet him. He embraced and kissed his son as he allowed himself to operate in the divine love that had been shed abroad in his heart. This is love in action and it is worthy of our imitation.

The forgiving love of the father symbolizes the divine mercy of God. Our heavenly Father always tempers judgment with mercy and does not deal with us using fear but love. While I am not attempting to add or delete anything from the Bible, I think this parable may be appropriately entitled 'The Parable of the Father's Love" rather than "The Prodigal Son." It shows a contrast between the self-centerd exclusiveness of the Pharisees, who failed to understand God's love, and the joy of God at the repentance of sinners.

Love is at the heart of Jesus' teaching. He teaches us to follow His example by being kind to the ungrateful and to those with evil intent. In Luke 6:35-36, Jesus instructs us to love our enemies, do good to them, and lend to them without expecting to get anything back. He then assures us that as we obey the most important command we will be rewarded bountifully as He qualifies us to be called sons of the Most High. This is because our Father is also kind to the ungrateful and wicked, and He shows mercy to the merciless.

When Jesus was asked to identify the greatest commandment, He said, "Love the Lord your God with all your heart and with all your soul and with all your mind and with all your strength" (Mark 12:30).

God has no desire to share our love with any of the little gods of this world. He makes this clear in the Book of Deuteronomy: "For the LORD your God is a consuming fire, a jealous God" (Deuteronomy 4:24).

Giving God the fullness of our love requires that we live a dedicated and holy life: "But just as he who called you is holy, so be holy in all you do" (1 Peter 1:15).

Our love must be intently focused on the holy things of God rather than on the corrupted things of this world. If ever we allow our love for God to mix with our love for the world, the worldly love will initially dilute and can eventually replace the love we have for God.

WHAT IS LOVE?

Love has many different meanings. When we say "I love you" to our spouse, parents, children, families, friends, or country, we usually mean something different in each instance. The word can describe a sexual desire; or, it can describe positive feelings between parents and children, and between members of a family.

The *Longman Modern English Dictionary* defines love as "a powerful emotion felt for another person manifesting itself in deep affection, devotion or sexual desire." This tells us that to love someone is to hold that person dear in our hearts—to appreciate people, to cherish them, dote on them, have affection for them, and to be in a deep emotional relationship with them. We shall explore the different meanings of love as follows.

In his book *The Four Loves*, C.S. Lewis divides human love into many different categories. My focus here will be on the four categories that are used in the Greek tradition (and which therefore appear in the New Testament Scriptures).

1. Storge (pronounced STOR-gay)

This describes affection between members of a family, for example between parents and children. Parental love is the first love a child experiences and the first love he or she understands. In fact, parental love is often the means by which children actually open themselves to God's love and come to understand it early in life. This love can also be extended toward non-family members—the main criterion is a comfortable familiarity with the person because we have known them for a long time and are fond of them or something about them.

This type of affection is usually expressed in a comfortable, private, and quiet context. These people provide us with a large share of our happiness on this earth, but we need to guard against misusing our affections to overwhelm the recipient to the extent that love turns into hate. In one of her books, Stormie Omartian suggests that from the time our children are born, we should pray, "God help me to really love my child the way you want me to and teach me how to show it in a way he (she) can understand." I say a resounding "Amen" to that prayer.

2. Philia (pronounced fee-LEE-ah)

The verb *philia* (friendship) in Greek is more naturally used to describe intimate affection. It is used in John 11:3 and 11:36 to give us an indication of how deeply Jesus loved Lazarus. Jesus' love was so evident that the Jews had to comment in verse 36, "See how he loved him!" Jesus revealed His love for Lazarus by raising him from the position of defeat (death) and giving him a new lease of life. We also see Jesus' love *(philia)* for mankind revealed through His countless acts of compassionate healing. Examples may be found in Mark 1:41 (healing a man with leprosy) and Luke 7:13-14 (where Jesus raises a widow's son from the dead).

While lovers are normally absorbed face-to-face in each other, and friends live side-by-side and are absorbed in some common interest, God is *eternally* absorbed in and with us. *Philia* is the least natural of the loves, the least instinctive, organic, or biological and the least necessary because we can live and breed without friendship. That is one of the reasons friendship love is the least appreciated in our modern society. Two people who fall in love and are sexually active may become friends, as well as lovers, because they have discovered a common interest they shared with one another that is not rooted in erotic love. CS Lewis believes the pleasure of friendship is greatest when each brings out all that is best, wisest, and/or funniest in others. But he warns against people joining together for reasons other than shared interests, as this creates elite groups and may cause others to rush to join a group because of the fear of being left outside. This in turn may destroy the original foundation of the friendships.

3. Agape (pronounced ah-GAH-pay)

The word *agape* in Greek expresses the highest and noblest form of love that sees something infinitely precious in its object. This is the kind of love one has toward God. It is a kind of love God has for us and is good in all circumstances. In the New Testament, Jesus gives us the two greatest commandments, "Love the Lord your God with all your heart," and "Love your neighbor as yourself" (Mark 12:30-31).

The word for love in both commandments is a verb based on *agape*. This type of love is not based on feelings but on the will. We make a conscious decision to love, irrespective of any unpleasant actions or reactions from others. It is the kind of love that makes you will the best for someone and act accordingly, even toward a person you dislike. *Agape* love helps us to reverse negative feelings to positive ones—for example, if we inadvertently help someone we do not like; we tend to dislike them less.

Agape is the key to all successful relationships. It was this sacrificial and unconditional love that enabled the Father to sacrifice His only Son for our sinful world. Romans 5:8 tells us, "But God shows and clearly proves His (own) love for us by the fact that while we were still sinners, Christ (the Messiah, the Anointed One) died for us" (Amplified Version).

Agape is all-giving without seeking a return. God's love is higher, deeper, truer, and based on self-giving. Its value increases with the passing of time as we go deeper in our walk with God.

4. Eros (pronounced EH-ros)

Eros describes a romantic love between people who are *in love*. It is the kind of love that exists between husband and wife, and it is sexual in nature. It is usually based on feelings and extends beyond friendship and affection. Without *eros,* none of us would have been born; and without affection none of us would have been reared. *Eros* love enables lovers to be deeply absorbed in each other, exploring the work of a very creative God.

It is important to note that God calls us to meet our spouse's love-needs and to consider the needs of "the other half" as being more important than our own. When we do this wholeheartedly, each loving and focusing on meeting the legitimate needs of the other, the relationship is strengthened, and we are winning in our desire to build a strong foundation for a great marriage.

I strongly urge any couples reading this book not to use sex as a weapon to punish your partners. If you do this, you run the risk of losing your spouse to another man or woman, another project, or simply to your children because the love-vacuum unwittingly created will need to be filled by someone or something else. By meeting your partner's love-needs, you are also strengthening your marriage against temptation.

Eros love may cause emotional attachment, jealousy, an unimaginable level of happiness, and a state of bliss for a short period, which may quickly fade away if it is not accompanied by affection and friendship. In its negative form, *eros* love may seek to conquer, possess, or use whatever tools possible to achieve a pleasurable moment. It is sometimes demanding and always in a hurry.

True love demands that we offer to our spouse the following: unconditional love and acceptance, sexual intimacy, spiritual intimacy, emotional intimacy and communication, companionship, encouragement, and affirmation. Love goes beyond feelings. It is a deep affection that drives us to care profoundly for someone else. It is also a commitment to act and to actively pursue the best for our loved ones. It involves self-sacrifice irrespective of our feelings and emotions.

According to Jay E. Adams, one definition of love based on the biblical teaching is: "the fulfilment of God's commandments, a responsible relationship to God and to man." Adams goes on to say that love is a relationship conditioned by responsibility—that is, responsible observance of the commandments of God.

THE BENCHMARK OF LOVE

Jesus gave us a benchmark of love by dying for us all while we were still sinners. His sacrifice on the Cross, suffering for mankind, triumph over man's enemy, resurrection from the dead, ascension, and continual regeneration of our lives by His Spirit all point to the undeniable fact that God is love. Jesus lived His life for one purpose—to offer His life in sacrifice for our sins so that all who believe in Him can be eternally restored to the Father (John 3:16).

God wants us to love others primarily because He loves everyone and desires His love to be expressed through us. He gave us a natural capacity to love and instructed us to be living expressions of love. Those who have accepted this foundational truth and are committed to walking in it regularly see this love operating in their lives beyond human comprehension. They are now free to embrace people as their brothers and sisters without earthly inhibitions.

In 1 John 4:18, John defines fear and love as being mutually exclusive. Love is from God and whoever lives in love lives in God; and fear is from Satan, because it has to do with punishment or condemnation. Violence and aggression are unlikely to cast out fear but may actually be a trigger for more violence, which accentuates the fears in people's minds. The good news is that we have the assurance of God's love, which erases all fear. This tells us that the only way to 'put off' fear is to put on love. From the above we are able to infer that a way to cast out fear is to learn more perfectly how to love. It sounds so simple, yet many are still struggling in this area of love.

If we are really to walk in love, we need to adjust the way we relate to one another, be sensitive to the needs of others, and stop using fear in our relationships. Instead, study the methods used by Jesus to relate to the rich, poor, sinners, and men and women alike. When Nicodemus came seeking Jesus in the night, Jesus simply told him the truth about salvation. He had dinner with the sinful tax collectors; He ministered to the sinful woman at the well and refused to condemn the woman caught in the act of adultery. He got His message across to them without alienating them. As a result they came to believe in Him and to rank highly among His most ardent followers.

When we grasp the fact that God is love, we will rise above the level of being insensitive people, unconscious of our use of fear, which can prevent us from really showing the love of Christ to the world. We need to begin to associate in our minds the idea of love and of God. The Apostle Paul caught this revelation in 1 Corinthians 13 and declared that whatever tremendous and impressive things he may have accomplished, however wide and deep his knowledge, however strong his faith, if he had no love, he amounted to nothing. This passage was written by Paul to teach us about how we are to love one another. But it also serves to teach us about the nature and character of God's love for us. We can only love others because He first loved us in this way.

According to 1 John 5:3, loving God means keeping His commandments. We are able to obey His commands because of our new birth, and because the Holy Spirit enables us to obey. As the victory has been won for us, we are no longer bound to live sinfully; we now have the ability to move from fear to love. "The goal of this command is love, which comes from a pure heart and a good conscience and a sincere faith" (1 Timothy 1:5).

Our goal for preaching and counseling should include, among other things, the desire to foster love toward God as He first loved us, and toward our neighbors. Thus, God's love expressed on the Cross becomes the standard by which fear is confronted, especially the fear of change. Love provides the means of personal transformation toward the freedom of consciousness. The liberation from sin is only one of the consequences—not the fruit of saintliness in the sense of a recompense for one's obedience—of the divine love. Anything short of ministering and relating to each other in love is inconsistent with Scripture.

When we love people, we want to show them that we care, spend time with them, and just be close to them. Simply put, we want to have a relationship with them. However, it takes two for a relationship to work. Just as we want our partners and friends to respond to our love, so God's love also demands a response from us. We need to allow our spirits to become aligned with His, and then we can begin a wonderful relationship that fear cannot break.

It is hard to be full of God's love and still be selfish or have a desire to put people under the bondage of fear. When we are full of His love,

God will sometimes move us to do things that are outside our comfort zone. The Bible assures us of God's love, and the Holy Spirit helps to circulate that love throughout our system—as we see what Jesus sees we are able to go beyond the call of duty to show someone God's nature through our actions. To demonstrate how love conquers fear, I have reproduced below a couple of stories from Jay E. Adams.

STORY 1—THE MOTHER AND THE LITTLE BOY IN DANGER[1]

A little boy went for a swim in the small lake behind his house. He jumped into the water, not realizing that as he swam toward the middle of the lake an alligator was swimming toward him.

Looking out of the window, the boy's mother saw the two as they got closer and closer together. In utter fear, she ran toward the water, yelling to her son as loudly as she could. Hearing her voice, the little boy became alarmed and made a U-turn to swim to his mother. It was too late. Just as he reached her, the alligator reached him. From the dock, the mother grabbed her little boy by the arms just as the alligator snatched his legs. There was an incredible tug-of-war between the two.

Although the alligator was much stronger than the mother, the mother was too passionate to let go. A farmer heard her screams, raced from his truck with his gun, took aim, and shot the alligator. The boy survived with two deep scars—one from the alligator, and the other from his mother's fingernails that had dug into his flesh in her efforts to hang onto the son she loved.

Like the mother, God has refused to let us go. He is also willing and able to save us. He has saved us from the enemy's clutches because of His love for us. The woman in question forgot her fears; she let perfect love cast out all her fears.

Story 2 — A Man with a Phobia of Crossing Bridges[2]

In his book *The Christian Counselor's Manual*, Jay Adams tells the story of a man with a phobia of crossing bridges. Upon hearing of a road accident involving his children, this man drove heedlessly over two bridges to reach them, experiencing no fear whatsoever in the process. Apparently, a few days before the incident, he had refused to cross those very same bridges. This is the power of love that casts out fear. Such love enabled our Lord Jesus to endure the Cross in order to save us. I am personally indebted to Jesus for His finished work on the Cross. Are you?

Love from God and for God erases all fear, as the Scripture puts it, "There is no fear in love. But perfect love drives out fear" (1 John 4:18).

At this point, let us go on a wonderful tour in a bid to understand the sources and effects of fear and love in our lives. This is not an exhaustive list, but it gives us a good idea of the kind of damage fear can wreak in our lives and how love can counteract its effects. Jesus' command to love our enemies (Matthew 5:44) is recognition that the only way to cope with our fears is to learn to overcome those fears through grace and love, however costly.

Fear and Love Compared

At this point, let us go on a wonderful tour in a bid to understand the sources and effects of fear and love in our lives.

FEAR	LOVE
Fear involves impending punishment.	There is no fear in love.
Fear is negatively contagious.	Love is positively contagious.
Fear is from the enemy of God.	Love is from the heart of the Father.

The purpose of fear is to imprison our mind.

Love sets our mind free.

Fear is the opposite of faith, and anyone who entertains fear cannot please God.

Love is derived from faith in the Lord, and we please Him when we put our faith in God.

Fear turns us away from God.

Love draws us closer to God.

Fear sometimes results from our sin.

Love results from recognizing the finished work on the Cross.

Fear makes us move away from problems or people, and by so doing we allow the problem to grow deeper.

Love makes us to move toward the problem or person, and our vulnerable position allows God to give us a divine solution to the problem.

Fear intimidates and taunts us.

Love throws the hand of God around the intimidated and brings comfort from the throne of mercy.

Fear is self-protecting.

Love is self-giving. Love keeps no record of our past failures or wrongdoings.

Fear reminds us of our past failures and their consequences.

Love keeps no record of our past failures or wrongdoings.

A fearful teacher is terrified of the consequences of rebuking an unruly pupil.

A teacher filled with love will discipline the unruly child in love.

Fear of the audience or unhealthy concern for self can lead to stage fright.

Love for the audience and the thought of God's faithfulness removes unhealthy fear.

Fear uses manipulation to the detriment of the sufferer.

Love encourages and challenges for the benefit of the sufferer.

Fear is suspicious of others, and it asks, "What will he do to me?"	Love looks for the opportunity to give and asks, "What can I do for you?"
Fear fails to undertake responsibilities today because it has fears about tomorrow.	Love labors doing today's task, and it has no time to worry about tomorrow.
Fear leads to greater fear, since failure to assume responsibility brings additional fear of the consequences of acting irresponsibly.	Love leads to greater love, which in turn brings joy, peace, and satisfaction.

This is not an exhaustive list, but it gives us a good idea of the kind of damage fear can wreak in our lives and how love can counteract its effects.

Let us fear the Lord, delight in His commandments, and watch Him cast out all our unhealthy fears with His loving hand. His love is unwavering, His covenant eternal, and His promises sure. God's love is part of His personality. It cannot be swayed by passion or diverted by disobedience because His love is everlasting. Israel's unfaithfulness could have no lasting effect upon God's love as the Lord declares through the prophet Jeremiah, "I have loved you with an everlasting love; I have drawn you with loving-kindness. I will build you up again and you will be rebuilt, O Virgin Israel" (Jeremiah 31:3-4).

It is, however, worth noting that in spite of God's love, our disobedience or unfaithfulness to Him may lead us to unnecessary pain and defeat; but God is always willing to restore in remembrance of Jesus' sacrifice on the Cross.

The Scriptures tell us that nothing casts out fear like perfect love. As an illustration of this assertion and using Story 1 above, Jay E. Adams puts it this way, "A mother is not immobilized by the fear of a wild animal attacking the child that she loves. Foolishly or otherwise, her love overcomes fear and casts it out as she throws herself into the fray."[3] He concludes by saying that love therefore demonstrates itself as greater than fear.

Again, in Story 2 above, Jay E. Adams talks about a man with a phobia for crossing bridges who overcame this problem through the strength of his love—in order to save his children. The question in my mind surrounding this story is: "What changed in this man?" The answer is rooted in the man's love for his children. Like our heavenly Father, this father would do anything to ensure the safety of his children. During his unselfish act, he receives a divine cure for his phobia. In fact, he did not remember anything about his fear for crossing bridges at the time; otherwise he may have panicked and stopped. But perfect love for his children cast out his fears. Perfect love led to deliverance without anyone laying hands on him. That is the work of our Father in Heaven whose compassion can minister equally to both believers and unbelievers.

As we recognize that God loved us first, by sending His only Son into this world as an atoning sacrifice for our sins, we are able to love Him back and also to extend that divine love to everyone around us. Our walk with the Lord enables us to grow in love, and this love produces faith and boldness to negate the fear in and around us. What am I saying here? I am simply establishing a fact: *The more we fear, the less we love; the more we love, the less we fear; but love conquers all fear.*

Love defines the character of God—His whole being is love. That is why John says, "Whoever does not love does not know God, for God is love" (1 John 4:8).

Love and Temptation

As we are beginning to realize the truth about love and familiarize ourselves with the personality of love as described by the Apostle Paul in 1 Corinthians 13, most of us may now attempt to walk in the most excellent way—that is, the way of love. In our bid to walk in love, it is important to recognize certain temptations that may come our way.

1. The Temptation to Imitate Love

We only grow in character if we are real and honest with ourselves. By that I mean not acting as loving Christians for a while only to turn back to our old ways when that love is being tested. If we cannot love the unlovable, it is better to admit our shortcomings and turn to God for help in prayer so that by His Spirit we may produce the genuine fruit of love. We cannot imitate love and behave kindly, justly, and sensitively toward one another without giving of ourselves which is the essence of love. We may fail to do this because subconsciously we are afraid of being hurt, thereby missing the opportunity for 'real' love instead of living with a poor imitation of love.

2. The Temptation to Hate Oneself

This may occur when we are confronted with the truth and we become disgusted and dispirited to find how self-loving and self-centerd our life really is. The self with whom we have lived for some years in reasonable comfort may become an intolerable person, and before long we may have slipped into despising ourselves wholeheartedly. The effect of this can be devastatingly contagious as the man who despises or hates himself will sooner or later reveal hatred and contempt for his fellow human beings. Irrespective of his profession of love for sinners, the contempt for the sin that he has found in himself is all too easily projected onto those who sin. Someone well-meaning but honestly wrong may say, "Did Jesus not say a man should deny himself?" (Mark 8:34). Yes, He did. But the purpose of His statement is to challenge us to voluntary self-giving to others, not self-contempt. We are not to hate ourselves—anyone advocating that we should hate ourselves is just being used as Satan's instrument without knowing it. The Bible simply promotes admitting our faults in the presence of God so that we can move on and do great exploits for God. God does not wait for our perfection before using us; otherwise, no one would qualify.

3. The Temptation to Separate the Love of God from the Love of People

In his book *New Testament Christianity* (1956), J.B. Phillips said, "It is easier to love a dog who more than rewards us by the utmost fidelity and affection, than it is to love people who in addition to being much more complex beings often do not reward us at all." Similarly, it is easy to love humanity without loving people. Many of the greatest crimes against individuals living today have been committed in the name of love for God and humanity. An example of this crime is the incident at the Twin Towers in New York City on September 11, 2001, which took many people's lives prematurely under the pretext of fighting for the liberty of certain groups of people. The perpetrators of such crimes conveniently forget (or do not believe in) the eternal judgment that awaits anyone who takes the lives of others.

Jesus is well aware that people can be difficult to love, so He inextricably linked the love of God with the love of other people. We know that our God is holy, perfect, truthful, and loving. Such attributes make it easy to respond to Him with worship and adoration. Yet we find it difficult to comprehend that this very same God has joined himself through Christ with ordinary human beings. In the parable of the last judgment (or the sheep and the goats), Jesus says that our treatment of fellow human beings is judged to be the same thing as our treatment of Christ himself. He puts it this way: "For I was hungry and you gave me something [or nothing] to eat, I was thirsty and you gave me something [or nothing] to drink, I was a stranger and you invited [or did not invite] me in, I needed clothes and you clothed [or did not clothe] me, I was sick and you looked after [or did not look after] me" (Matthew 25:35-36; see also 25:42-43).

The above exhortation means that the way we treat other people is a certain indication of the way we treat Christ. I am very much aware that some people may not take kindly to this interpretation, but if we really allow the Holy Spirit of God to minister to us, the true picture will be revealed in our hearts. John supported this interpretation when he asked, "If a man say, I love God, and hateth his brother, he is a liar: for he that loveth not his brother whom he hath seen, how can he love God whom he hath not seen?" (1 John 4:20, KJV).

4. The Temptation to Feel that People Are Not Worth Loving

The world is lamentably short of releasing unselfish, unconditional love because some have tried loving others and have been sadly abused and mistreated. Too many of us have concluded that people are not really worth the effort. If you feel like this, please remember the sacrificial love of God in sending His only Son to die for us while we were still sinners. He could have rightly concluded that man was not worthy of the highest sacrifice. Instead He bore all misunderstanding and humiliation to win us to himself. John puts it succinctly, "Dear friends, since God so loved us, we also ought to love one another" (1 John 4:11).

Yes, people can be ignorant, selfish, rude, and irritating at the best of times. If we digest the truth that God has identified himself with man in Christ, then we see the force of John's question. Ironically, some modern, sophisticated Christians have separated the love of God from the love of their brothers and sisters. Whenever an individual turns a blind eye to the suffering of his fellow believer, this split occurs. Likewise, whenever the Church focuses solely upon itself and restricts her love to her own members and programs, this flaw is exposed.

May I remind those individuals or churches that salvation and the manifestation of God's Spirit in its purest form will only flow when the love of God goes hand-in-hand with the love of our fellow-men. To show brotherly love includes, among other things, genuine and lasting affection for one another (1 Peter 1:22), showing of hospitality to one another (Hebrews 13:1-2), offering help to needy Christians (1 John 3:17) that the world may know Him (John 13:35), and generally doing good to all (Galatians 6:10).

In 1 John 4:18, John points out that perfect love casts out fear. However it is also true that fear can cast out love if we have empowered anxieties, strife, envy, and suspicion and driven love and goodwill to the background of our lives. Most of us come up short in this and so need a fresh outpouring of God's love. But this love can only be received if we are willing to be open to God and are ready to cooperate with His purposes. Our love bank can only be filled and enriched when we surrender to the love of God, and remain in regular communion with Him.

The love of God is the only solution for dealing with our pride and prejudices. Fear will not be driven from our hearts by resolution only but by willingly receiving the very Spirit of Love. The Church must be conscious of and concerned about the needs of her people and let love for them galvanize her to action. As we strive to rid ourselves of fear, we realize that it is a mighty challenge, so we are driven back to God, who is love. It is only from Him that we can draw our supply of compassion and attitude of self-giving. It is Jesus who can transform us from being people with a limited ability to love into those who can feel real concern for the condition of others who are far outside our normal circle. It is through Jesus that we find courage to go into unpromising situations and see them redeemed through the power of His love.

Walking in Love

Here we are asking ourselves a simple question: What must be given or done in order for us to walk in love? For the purpose of this section, walking in love implies progress in a forward direction on a daily basis, which also means adopting the loving attitude Christ had embraced on behalf of the world. The greatest love story is that while we were still sinners, Christ died for us (Romans 5:8).

Salvation is a free gift, but it did not come cheap; it cost the blood of Jesus. When we receive Jesus Christ as our Lord and Savior, His love impacts our hearts through the Holy Spirit. We are then expected to impart and bring healing to others. But to walk in love has its price. The price of walking in godly love includes the following:

- being patient with others
- encouraging others
- building each other up
- bringing others closer to Jesus
- helping others when they need our help.

Walking in love may require us to respect others when we do not feel they deserve that respect. It may require us to trust a renewed or reformed person with our money or be ready to help others at uncomfortable or inconvenient times. It may entail caring for elderly parents or family members or working with an unbeliever who regularly tries our patience to the limit. Walking in love requires us to be tolerant and understanding with each other—more than what comes naturally to us, just as God is more understanding of our shortcomings than we deserve. We are required not just to love in words or speech but also in deed and truth (1 John 3:18).

Many gifts are available to Christians through the Holy Spirit, but God prefers that our top priority be love. Priority should be given to loving others, both within the Body of Christ and in the world at large (1 Corinthians 13:1-13). Based on Paul's admonition, we need to evaluate the quality of our love and ask ourselves the following questions:

- Am I kind, even when others are not?
- Am I easily angered, and do I keep a log-book of the wrongs done to me?
- Am I envious of other people's achievements?
- Am I always looking to see the best in people?
- Do I exercise patience when others are being difficult?
- Do I treat people rudely?
- Do I always want to get my own way?
- Do I use manipulation or threats to control a person's life?
- Do I tell the truth, even when it is disadvantageous to me?
- Do I believe in people even when they do not believe in me?
- Do I persevere in the face of antagonism and love people who make my life difficult?

An honest evaluation and answer to each of the above should reveal areas in which God is calling us to change. The Bible tells us that the day we become born again God pours out His love into our hearts through His Holy Spirit (Romans 5:5). However, walking in love is not automatic when you become a Christian. It requires discipline, resolution, commitment, and the help of the Holy Spirit. Communicating with God is the anchor to walking in love. Spending time in God's presence helps to build our love and confidence in Him; through this practice we are then equipped to walk in love and power.

First Thessalonians 5:17 encourages us to pray continually. When we do this, it strengthens our relationship with God, whose nature is love. As sons of God, we inherit His nature by blood lineage, and when we walk in love we keep the communication lines open for impartation. This relationship will be of benefit to us when we face difficulties because our prayers will not be filled with a sense of panic but with the confidence that we know our Father, and that His will for us is good and not evil.

Ephesians 5:1-2 admonishes us to be imitators of God by walking in love, just as Christ also loved us and gave himself up for us. This calls us to sacrificial love for one another. It also challenges us to deny our own comfort by reducing optional activities in order to meet the urgent needs of others.

HELPING OTHERS MOVE FROM FEAR TO LOVE

"The more we fear, the less we love; the more we love, the less we fear; but love conquers all fear." —Akeem Shomade

The above quote is a good basis with which to start a counseling session for someone struggling in the area of fear and love. We need to be filled with love for other people's sake and to avoid making premature judgments or ill-informed conclusions. Because of our perfect love for others, the Lord will speak through us and bring solution and breakthrough into the situations at hand.

Those who desire to help other people must seek God's guidance in determining the sources of a person's fear and how to minister sensitively the call to repentance and love. We need to ask questions such as: "Is the fear basically a fear of God, a fear of man, or the work of the enemy?" If the person we are helping fears God, then we need to explore his/her relationship with God. We may want to establish whether he/she genuinely believes and understands the biblical teachings about assurance and peace. As we know that light and darkness cannot dwell together. We also need to assess the possibilities for sin in the person's life that the enemy could be feeding upon to disrupt his or her relationship with God.

If there is known sin in people's lives, we need to remind them of God's promises in Deuteronomy 28:58-68. We should tell them what the results of sin are (which come from not carefully following the words of the Lord as written in His Word). We should let the person know that sickness, anxiety, weariness, a despairing heart, and fear could all come as the effects of sin not repented. God is not the author of fear, but sometimes He can allow a spirit of fear to come upon His children if we have turned away from Him and He wants to discipline us in love. If the Lord allows a spirit of fear to torment us, we need a genuinely repentant heart and the renewal of a loving relationship with Him. These come when we rededicate our lives to the Lord.

At this point we need to remember that we reap what we sow in the flesh. However, God's love for us and His forgiveness were not dependent upon our repentance. It was while we were still sinners that He died for us. All sin—past, present and future—was forgiven unconditionally at the Cross of Calvary. Although we should remember that sin of which we are unrepentant can get in the way of our receiving the abundant life God desires for us.

If people's fear can be referred to as the fear of man, then we may encourage them to engage in loving ministry to others. This means allowing the love of God to be pre-eminent in our lives so that we can be life givers to others. By giving ourselves to others, we allow God's perfect love to drive out all our fears. Thus, where we have operated in fear we then begin to operate in love instead. However, it must be emphasized that we should guard against improper motives—we must not minister to others in order to meet our own need (the need to love and to be needed) as God does not respect such services.

We need to challenge people with God's Word. For example, Isaiah 57:11 says, "Whom have you so dreaded and feared that you have been false to me, and have neither remembered me nor pondered this in your hearts? Is it not because I have long been silent that you do not fear me?"

This is a direct challenge to those Jews who dreaded the power and idle threats of men rather than fearing God. It applies to us, too. We need to examine ourselves. Is it because the Holy Spirit is such a gentleman and does not fill our lives with empty noise but only a quiet whisper, that we sometimes fear Him less than man? Is it because the Lord is so gracious as to allow us freedom of choice when man sometimes does not? Would we rather trade on His grace than face the consequences of standing up to man and his schemes? Remember that God is love, and He is aware of our weaknesses, which is why He paid the ultimate price through the death of His only Son. He also assures salvation to any (not only Jews) who repent, confess their sin, and place their faith in Jesus.

In Isaiah 57:11-12, the prophet speaks firmly against the Jews because they were destitute of the fear of God, though they boasted of their holiness and (empty) religion. Isaiah called them hypocrites who flattered themselves in their superstition. Yet they acted haughtily and insolently toward God and man. The prophet declares that true fear of God cannot exist where the worship is not pure and consistent with His Word.

In verse 12 of this chapter, Isaiah affirms that the Lord will no longer endure what He formerly endured, and that the people must turn back from their wicked deeds and unrighteous ways in order to enter into a full relationship with Him. The fact that we are now under the new covenant of grace should not be taken as an excuse to continue in sin. God is not mocked.

We must let our fear of man diminish as we substitute fear with love; we must respect and cherish men but direct our adoration toward God. God wants us to love others primarily because He loves them and desires His love to be expressed through us. God shed His love abroad in our hearts and gave us the gift of the Holy Spirit as an assurance of His love. The gift of His Son Jesus Christ is God's ultimate expression of His love for us. Let us use the weapon of love to attack our fear of helping people and be assured that the Lord remembers us when we remember others. He rewards us for showing kindness to others and giving practical help.

A Practical Lesson in Love

To support the points made above and to show how love crowds out fears, I would like to share a story with you. It is called "Smile—Breakfast at McDonald's" (author unknown).

A sociology tutor asked a mother of three children in her last year of studying, along with others, to go and smile at three people and documents their reactions. Being a very friendly person, this lady set out for McDonald's with her husband and their three children. Hoping to share a special moment with her family, they were soon standing in line waiting to be served when all of a sudden everyone around them began to back away, including her husband. She did not move an inch, although an overwhelming feeling of panic welled up inside of her as she turned to see why everyone had moved.

As she turned around, a horrible dirty body smell greeted her, and there standing behind her were two poor homeless men. One of them was short and had a smile on his face. The man's eyes were sky blue and full of God's light as he searched for acceptance. He said, "Good day" as he counted the few coins he had been clutching. The second man was mentally challenged, and the blue-eyed man was his support. The young lady at the counter asked what they wanted, and he said, "Coffee is all, Miss." That was all they could afford, and if they wanted to sit in the restaurant and warm up, they had to buy something. They just wanted to be warm.

Our final year student and mother of three children smiled and asked for two extra breakfast meals on a separate tray, which she then gave to the two homeless people. The blue-eyed man looked up at her with tears in his eyes and said, "Thank you." She leaned over, began to pat his hand, and said, "I did not do this for you. God is here working through me to give you hope."

The lady cried as she walked away to join her family. They held hands for a moment, knowing that it was only because of God's grace that they had been able to give. That day showed them the pure light of God's love.

Our lesson from the above story is one of unconditional acceptance. We should learn how to love people and use things—not love things and use people. Perfect love cast out this woman's fears as she could see the homeless people from God's perspective rather than from the world's standards. More importantly, it is worth mentioning that love has its price. It cost our Father His beloved Son, Jesus Christ; He in turn willingly gave His life because of His unconditional love for us. For our student in the above story, it cost her money, her time, the separating of herself from the crowd, her mixed emotions, perseverance, panic, anxiety, the inhaling of smelly body odor, and obedience to the prompting of the Holy Spirit.

In other words, love enables us to suffer ridicule and pain, to embrace the Cross of Christ, and to love the unlovable, which includes loving those who hate us and have been horrible to us in every way we can imagine. There is always a price to pay in love; it could be time, money, patience, or bearing false accusations or insults. When we can love the unlovable, we bring alive the Scripture that says that perfect love casts out fears (1 John 4:18). Remember that "God is love. Whoever lives in love lives in God, and God in him. In this way, love is made complete among us so that we will have confidence on the day of judgment, because in this world we are like him" (1 John 4:16-17).

The Benefits of Walking in Love

Love is not a choice but an extension of who we are. In today's world most of us have been programmed to assess our reason for doing certain things, re-evaluate, consider the advantages, and ask ourselves questions like:"What's in it for me?" Below is a mouthwatering list of just some of the benefits of walking in love. These are examples and not an exhaustive list.

Love will set you free from unnecessary stress.

A deep, settled joy and peace will come upon you because it is impossible to walk in love and remain miserable. The psalmist says, "Yea, though I walk through the valley of the shadow of death, I will fear no evil: for thou art with me" (Psalm 23:4, KJV).

By walking regularly in forgiveness and not counting up the evils done to you, you can live a more stress-free existence. Living with less stress uplifts the quality of your health. Just imagine no headaches, migraines, or backaches, no emotional turmoil or spiritual leakage. Remember that love is not fretful or resentful; it keeps no record of the evil done to it (1 Corinthians 13:4-5).

A quality prayer life.

Your prayer life will be enhanced because you are aligning your spirit with God's Spirit to minister into situations out of compassion, love, and in His direction. You therefore have a right standing with God because you are operating under His direction in His realm. The more loving you are, the more like Him you become because love is His nature. Remember, Jesus still set aside time to fellowship in prayer with the Father (Luke 6:12-13). Your attitude to prayer may reveal how much you really love God, although it is not the only yardstick for measuring love for God.

You will receive the divine ability to focus on the needs of others and give them precedence.

Love will cost you time, money, and your natural preoccupation with self. Instead of always receiving, you will become a giver; instead of condemning your enemies, you will begin to love and pray for them. Remember: "Be imitators of God, therefore, as dearly loved children and live a life of love, just as Christ loved us and gave Himself up for us as a fragrant offering and sacrifice to God" (Ephesians 5:1-2). John tells us how to do this in 1 John 3:11-24. Love for God will give you the ability to walk in accordance with and be guided by His commandments.

God has given you His love manual in the form of the Holy Bible; your part of the deal is to operate in line with Scripture so that you are simply walking in love. By making Jesus Christ your Lord and Savior, you have already taken one step of obedience and the love of God has been born in you. To sharpen this love-gift, you must take steps to develop it daily by remaining in fellowship with God through prayer and reading the Word of God. Choose to be a channel of love today and walk with God. Remember: "We know that we have come to know him if we obey his commands. The man who says, 'I know him,' but does not do what he commands is a liar, and the truth is not in him. But if anyone obeys his word, God's love is truly made complete in him" (1 John 2:3-5).

Look at John's description of how we know when we are living in Him: "This is how we know we are in him: Whoever claims to live in him must walk as Jesus did" (1 John 2:5-6).

John echoes this again in 2 John 1:6 when he teaches us that to love is to walk in obedience to His commands; and His command is that we walk in love (c.f. Matthew 22:26-40).

Love will give you a firm foundation.

If we love one another as commanded, we are like a man who built his house by digging deep, laying the foundation on a rock. Jesus is our Rock. His nature is love. All He did for mankind is only possible through love. A commitment to building everything we have upon the Rock of love offers us in return a stability and depth that the storms of life cannot blow away. We can enjoy the assurance that God is love, and love never fails. Always remember: "Love never fails. But where there are prophecies, they will cease; where there are tongues, they will be stilled; where there is knowledge, it will pass away" (1 Corinthians 13:8).

Also, Jesus told us in Luke 6:47-48 that if we hear and do His Word, we are like men who build their houses on a rock that the floods and storms of life cannot shake.

Love, faith and obedience ensure that nothing hinders your anointing.

The more you walk in love, the freer you are from fear, and that allows a free-flow of the anointing and power God has put in your life. The absence of fear also enables the full manifestation of this anointing by the Holy Spirit. The Lord is well aware of the crippling effect of fear, so He always tells His chosen vessels to "fear not" before commissioning them for a big task. In the Gospels, Jesus used the words 'fear not' to build up Jairus' faith just before He raised Jairus' daughter from the dead (Luke 8:50). Jesus knew that fear would contaminate Jairus' faith and block the free flow of the anointing. Remember, the only thing that counts is faith expressing itself through love (Galatians 5:6). Don't be afraid; just believe (Luke 8:50).

OTHER BENEFITS OF WALKING IN LOVE

• A growth in grace and absolute dependence on God, for it takes the power of the Holy Spirit for us to consistently walk in love.

• Growth in the knowledge of the Lord. When we know Him personally, we will experience His awesome power that enables us to love the unlovable.

• A witness for God. By virtue of our love for God and for other people, we are perfectly positioned to become effective witnesses for Jesus Christ and to minister in a non-judgmental manner. In doing this, we are preaching the gospel without using words.

• We receive the ability to forgive others. By virtue of our love for others and growth in the knowledge of the Lord, we become merciful like Jesus, who even on the Cross was able to pray for His persecutors, "Father, forgive them, for they do not know what they are doing" (Luke 23:34). The life of a person who walks in love will not be marked by unlimited violence, but by unlimited compassion and forgiveness. Jesus invoked God's forgiveness even for those who executed him.

Through love, Jesus took our pain and infirmities. He "was crushed for our iniquities; the punishment that brought us peace was upon him, and by his wounds we are healed" (Isaiah 53:5).

The spirit of fear cannot take away the effect of Christ's finished work in our lives; we are free to love the Lord with all our mind and soul and to love other people unconditionally.

Through unconditional love, we do not need to submit to empty, self-centerd, and worldly ways. Instead, we submit to Jesus and have unlimited access to His *agape* love. *Agape* is love that is unchanging and wants the very best for others. It never seeks to manipulate or control. This is the kind of love that is rich enough to cast out all fears. The Bible tells us that love should be given the topmost priority over other virtues in our Christian living (Ephesians 3:17-18; 4:2 and John 3:16).

Are we are able to confess that God is the one whom we love above all others, knowing that love requires that we be willing to suffer, even the cost of reaching out to our sworn enemies? If we love Him above all others, we can learn to live free of fear by learning and relearning what it means to be shaped by practices that immerse us in the patterns of God's love. This leads us to the crucified and risen Christ. To know Him is to obey Him, and to obey Him is to love Him.

In the outstretched arms of Jesus on the Cross, we see the width and depth and height of a love that is beyond our measuring—a love that meets and defeats evil and declares, *"I love you all, come to me and partake in my victory."* To enjoy the benefits of this unconditional love, we must know and believe who we are in Christ and resolve to walk in this. We must walk in love in order to walk in the anointing and power of God.

And for those who do not know this love and would like to have a personal relationship with Jesus, I suggest that you turn immediately to Appendix 1, which is located at the back of this book. Locate and pray a prayer of confession and ask Jesus to come and be your Lord and Savior. After your prayer, come back to this page to find out who you are in Christ Jesus.

This brings me to the importance of recognizing who I am in Christ. While writing this book, I had the opportunity of attending a discipleship counseling seminar led by Neil Anderson. I was really blessed and reminded of my freedom in Christ Jesus. Among other things, I was reminded by Pastor Anderson that:

- I am God's child (John 1:12).
- I have been justified through faith in Jesus Christ (Romans 5:1).
- I am united with the Lord, and I am one in spirit with Him (1 Corinthians 6:17).
- I am a member of Christ's Body (1 Corinthians 12:27).
- I am a saint (Ephesians 1:1).
- I have been adopted as God's child (Ephesians 1:5).
- I have direct access to God through the Holy Spirit (Ephesians 2:18).
- I have been redeemed and forgiven of all my sins (Colossians 1:14).
- I am complete in Christ (Colossians 2:10).

What a glorious privilege to be called sons of God and be imparted with such freedom in Christ! The ability to recognize who you are in Christ and to love yourself is critical to how you relate to others. That is the reason for the command to love your neighbors as you do yourself (Matthew 22:39). Fear has no place in a loving heart, just as light and darkness cannot co-exist. The tallest mountain in the world can be measured, but how can we measure the love of God? It is deeper, higher, and vaster than anything we know. Indeed, it cannot be compared with anything we know or have seen. Nothing can separate us from the love of Christ (Romans 8:35).

PRAYER

Like the Apostle Paul, "I pray that you, being rooted and established in love, may have power, together with all the saints, to grasp how wide and long and high and deep is the love of Christ, and to know this love that surpasses knowledge—that you may be filled to the measure of all the fullness of God" (Ephesians 3:17-19). Amen!

Bible Verses to Help Us

1. "There is no fear in love. But perfect love drives out fear, because fear has to do with punishmesnt. The one who fears is not made perfect in love" (1 John 4:18).
2. "Whoever does not love does not know God, because God is love" (1 John 4:8).
3. "For God so loved the world that he gave his one and only Son, that whoever believes in him shall not perish but have eternal life" (John 3:16).
4. "But God demonstrates his own love for us in this: While we were still sinners, Christ died for us" (Romans 5:8).
5. "How great is the love the Father has lavished on us, that we should be called children of God! And that is what we are" (1 John 3:1)!
6. "God is love. Whoever lives in love lives in God, and God in him. In this way, love is made complete among us so that we will have confidence on the day of judgment, because in this world we are like him" (1 John 4:16-17).
7. "Who shall separate us from the love of Christ? Shall trouble or hardship or persecution or famine or nakedness or danger or sword" (Romans 8:35)?
8. "As the Father has loved me, so have I loved you. Now remain in my love. If you obey my commands, you will remain in my love, just as I have obeyed my Father's commands and remain in his love" (John 15:9-10).
9. "Love the Lord your God with all your heart and with all your soul and with all your mind and with all your strength. The second is this: 'Love your neighbor as yourself.' There is no commandment greater than these" (Mark 12:30-31).
10. "Be completely humble and gentle; be patient, bearing with one another in love. Make every effort to keep the unity of the Spirit through the bond of peace" (Ephesians 4:2-3).

11. "Beloved, let us love one another: for love is of God; and every one that loveth is born of God, and knoweth God" (1 John 4:7, KJV).

12. "Dear friends, since God so loved us, we also ought to love one another" (1 John 4:11).

13. "Love must be sincere. Hate what is evil; cling to what is good. Be devoted to one another in brotherly love. Honor one another above yourselves" (Romans 12:9-10).

14. "I have loved you with an everlasting love; I have drawn you with loving-kindness. I will build you up again and you will be rebuilt, O Virgin Israel" (Jeremiah 31:3-4).

15. "If a man say, I love God, and hateth his brother, he is a liar: for he that loveth not his brother whom he hath seen, how can he love God whom he hath not seen" (1 John 4:20, KJV)?

16. "Dear children, let us not love with words or tongue but with actions and in truth" (1 John 3:18).

17. "Love is patient, love is kind. It does not envy, it does not boast, it is not proud. It is not rude, it is not self-seeking, it is not easily angered, it keeps no record of wrongs. Love does not delight in evil but rejoices with the truth. It always protects, always trusts, always hopes, always perseveres" (1 Corinthians 13:4-7).

18. "Be imitators of God, therefore, as dearly loved children and live a life of love, just as Christ loved us and gave himself up for us as a fragrant offering and sacrifice to God" (Ephesians 5:1-2).

19. "But if anyone obeys his word, God's love is truly made complete in him. This is how we know we are in him: Whoever claims to live in him must walk as Jesus did" (1 John 2:5-6).

20. "Love never fails. But where there are prophecies, they will cease; where there are tongues, they will be stilled; where there is knowledge, it will pass away" (1 Corinthians 13:8).

21. "The only thing that counts is faith expressing itself through love" (Galatians 5:6).

22. "He who loves Me will be loved by My Father, and I will love him and manifest Myself to him" (John 14:21, NKJV).

23. "A new command I give you: Love one another. As I have loved you, so you must love one another. By this all men will know that you are my disciples, if you love one another" (John 13:34-35).

End Notes

1. Email story, author unknown.
2. Adams, Jay. *The Christian Counselor's Manual*, (Page 415). Grand Rapids, Michigan: Zondervan Publishing House, 1973.
3. Adams, Jay. *The Christian Counselor's Manual*, (Page 415). Grand Rapids, Michigan: Zondervan Publishing House, 1973.

EIGHT

FEAR OF MAN[1]*

The purpose of this chapter is to expose the myth of man's perception of himself as self-important and to reinforce our earlier discussion relating to the fear of God. While some operate as God intended as rulers over creation, others abuse their delegated authority. Those who misuse their authority have not understood sufficiently the result of Adam's sin and as a result fail to enter into the finished work of Christ. Hence, man is forever manifesting the first Adam's sin.

Before we discuss the fear of man, I believe it is proper to provide an answer to the question: "Who is man?" I believe that when we see man with God's eye, we will easily be able to discern whether or not it is proper to fear man or God.

The *Longman Modern English Dictionary* describes man as "a member of a race of erect, biped mammals, with a highly developed brain, having the powers of articulate speech, abstract reasoning and imagination." The above definition tells us that man is unique and wonderfully made. However my next question is: "Wonderfully made by whom?" The quick answer from any believer would be; "By a wonderful and very creative God." Generally, you cannot give what you do not have. Blood cannot come out of a stone, and apples cannot grow on a banana tree or vice versa. I believe readers will agree with me that, in spite of what the evolutionists and some scientists say contrary to the biblical account, it takes a being with a highly developed faculty, a genius, to create the highly developed brain that man has been given. For the purpose of this book, I endorse the biblical creationist concept

---

1* The author uses "man" in its broadest context with no reference to gender

of man. Therefore, I use the word *man* in generic terms to describe the human being, both male and female.

The Structure of Man

According to the evolutionists, man is only an animal, a physical being, a product of the process of evolution. If this assertion is correct, my question is: "Who made the animals?" The Bible presents an altogether different and a more logical picture.

The Bible tells us that man is the handiwork of a creative God, a fact that evolutionists and advances in science cannot dispute without doing some violence to a number of facts in existence. Man is to possess the earth, bring it into submission, and rule over the other creatures (Genesis 1:26-27). It is emphasized throughout the Bible that man is part of nature, made from dust (Genesis 2:7). Although nature was made to serve him, man has to serve nature first by tending it and bringing it to fruition (Genesis 2:15). Man is created; he is not the Creator—and despite his highly developed brain, power of reasoning, and imagination, man is still limited when compared with God. For example, our DNA is highly complex and therefore the product of an extremely intelligent Design Engineer.

According to the Bible, Man cannot find the true meaning of his life within himself. He depends largely on social and physical interaction with the other elements of creation. And ultimately man needs God in order to maintain his existence, direction, and purpose (Genesis 2:18-25). Man is a spiritual being (*ruah* in Hebrew and *pneuma* in Greek) and has a body suit called flesh (*basar* in Hebrew and *sarx* in Greek), which covers his bones. He has a soul (*nepes* in Hebrew, but pronounced ne-fesh, no-fesh or na-fesh (*naf* in Arabic and *psyche* in Greek). He has feelings, varying emotions, and is endowed with the ability to make an informed choice. According to the Book of Ecclesiastes, some of man's emotions include the following: joy (2:10), love (9:1, 6, 9), hatred (2:17-18, 9:1-6), contentment (4:8), despair (2:20), and grief (2:23).

The use of the word *soul* throughout the Bible emphasizes man's individuality and vitality with emphasis on his inner life, feelings, and personal consciousness. Likewise the use of the word *body* may emphasize the historical and outward associations that affect his life. Man is also made like the Spirit of God in that he has a spirit, and yet not in such a way that he can be described as spirit alone. Man as flesh is man in his connection with the realm of nature and with humanity as a whole, not only in its weakness but also in its sinfulness and opposition to God.

The Bible tells us in the Book of Genesis that God created man in His own image and likeness (Genesis 1:27). This tells us that man is unique among the rest of creation and that with his power of reasoning and physical characteristics come responsibility toward his Creator. Man was given the stewardship of God's creatures. He is the man in charge and caretaker of this planet. "And God said, Let us make man in our image, after our likeness: and let them have dominion over the fish of the sea, and over the fowl of the air, and over the cattle, and over all the earth, and over every creeping thing that creepeth upon the earth" (Genesis 1:26, KJV).

In the above passage, man is given the highest authority as overseer of all God's creation. We are entitled to use this authority in accordance with His will for us, providing we do not take advantage of it. Examples of abuse of this position include ill-treating those whom God has placed under our care or tutelage, or hindering others from gaining a well-earned promotion. God has given man both a moral and rational nature. We can reason, distinguish between good and bad, worship, and explore like no other of God's creatures. God therefore expects us to respond personally to His gracious Word by operating in love, trust, and in relationship with Him in the position He has given us.

King Nebuchadnezzar took advantage of his position as ruler of Babylon. He was advised by God (through Daniel) to renounce his sins and receive God's grace and forgiveness. He would then have been able to rule over his territory in partnership with God. But the king did not renounce his ways and suffered the consequences. When we respond to a call for salvation or a direct word from God to turn from our wicked ways or to take a particular course of action, our obedience honors God. Our disobedience, if we so choose, brings with it negative consequences. King Nebuchadnezzar suffered untold hardship for his disobedience, abuse of power, and rejection of God's love—he lost his authority, his kingdom, and lived like a wild animal for many years (Daniel 4:31-37).

Although God made man to rule with Him, in comparison to Him we are highly insignificant! In Psalm 8:3-8, the psalmist (David), praises our Creator out of the wonder of His sovereign ordering of creation (see Genesis 1:26-28), concluding that humans are insignificant in comparison to God, as we are but specks of cosmic dust. Man was formed from the dust of the ground. But God has crowned man with an almost godlike glory (Genesis 1:26), given him the breath of life, and equipped him with a living soul. He has crowned man with His own glory and honor, just as a king crowns his son, the prince, and endows him with honor and power. The main purpose of this endowment was to give man the potential for fellowship with the lover of his soul. It is this relationship that lifts man above the rest of creation and confers on him the dignity of being a child of God, made in God's image and reflecting His glory.

Despite the power given to us, we need to remind ourselves that delegated authority is not absolute or independent power. It is rather a right given to us as we participate as subordinates in God's rule—and it is a gift, not a right to be abused. God loved man so much that He entrusted the whole earth and everything within it to his care. He put the Garden of Eden under man's care, and not the care of angels. Satan was so jealous that he plotted and succeeded in discrediting the first Adam. Job was so concerned about the attention God gives to man that he exclaimed, "What is man that you make so much of him, that you give him so much attention" (Job 7:17).

The answer to Job's lament could be found in creation, for we are created in God's image to have dominion over the world (Genesis 1:27-28).

In order to carry out this great commission on earth, we ought to confess our insignificance and depend solely on God's help. We should cast out self-deceptive spirits; put away anxiety, fear, inhibition, and alienation. We need to give God the glory due to Him and dissolve our man-made hero systems – that is, systems where we make ourselves demi-gods to be worshiped by all those who are put under our spiritual and natural cover.

DEFINING MAN FROM THE SCRIPTURES

We are about to take a tour of the Scriptures with the view to finding out what the Bible says about man:

- Man was made in God's image (Genesis 1:26).
- Man is the work of God, and he is wonderfully made (Psalm 139:14).
- God formed man from the dust of the ground (Genesis 2:7). Man has a spirit and soul as well as a physical body and as a result has been endowed with such characteristics as righteousness and holiness (Ephesians 4:24) and knowledge (Colossians 3:10).
- Because man is a spiritual being, he does not live on bread alone but on every word that comes from the mouth of God (Deuteronomy 8:3 and Matthew 4:4).
- God cares for man, and we are always on His mind (Psalm 144:3 and Psalm 8:4).
- Man was made from dust, and his body will return to dust (Psalm 90:3).
- Man is mortal, and his days on earth are normally limited to between 70-120 years (Psalm 90:10 and Genesis 6:3).
- Man no longer lives according to God's moral laws as His representatives on earth—we now have our own man-made codes of integrity (Psalm 12:1).
- The Lord directs a righteous man's steps, and we cannot understand His ways (Proverbs 20:24).
- "Cursed is the one who trusts in man, who depends on flesh for his strength and whose heart turns away from the LORD" (Jeremiah 17:5).
- "The man without the Spirit does not accept the things that come from the Spirit of God, for they are foolishness to him, and he cannot understand them" (1 Corinthians 2:14).
- Man needs to be on his guard, stand firm in his faith, and be of courage (1 Corinthians 16:13).
- Man is to be appreciated and not a power to be feared because he is made in the image of the true Lord who created everything—man, the stars, and the moon.

• Man, when he is regenerated, is God's temple, and God's Spirit lives in him (1 Corinthians 3:16).

The above list paints a scriptural picture of man and his character. It is true that all of God's creation was good and perfect. And that includes man, who later soiled the perfect nature with an imperfect act in the Garden of Eden. The Fall destroyed what was originally supernatural in man, so that the nature and image of God in him was damaged. Man was left with his free will to choose good or evil. God saw this and commented that "the man has now become like one of us, knowing good and evil" (Genesis 3:22).

This verse seems to imply that in man's refusal to obey God's command, man has taken to himself a right that God had withheld, and man's access to the knowledge of good and evil provided him with a status of divinity of some sort. But this view cannot be farther from the truth. It not only speaks of the reparation of the sin of man, but it also spells out the intention of God to restore man to his original status after the Fall. God does not want man to slide further. In fact, I may paraphrased the above passage like this: *Behold, man has become like one of us. He looks every bit a genius—so smart, so knowledgeable! Let us make sure he does not further undermine his condition by reaching out to the fruit of life and live a wretched life forever.*

This divine speech shows how low man has fallen from grace, but also the nature of the original sin that entered the world. In today's world, people are now actively deceiving one-another with the sole purpose of upstaging and gaining advantage each over the other. The root of fear, especially the fear of man, is the point at issue here.

What Is the Fear of Man?

Much has been written about man in the previous passages. We know that man has flesh and blood and that he is also a spiritual being. We know that his body can experience various emotions—joy, sadness, weariness, troubles, hatred, love, and contentment. Man has a soul, which functions as the center of his desires and the seat of inner satisfaction. God gave man a spirit to be used for relating to God. Man also has a mood or temperament and a conscience, which is part of his soul, telling him the difference between right and wrong.

The fear of man can be expressed as a reverential awe and regard of men or a blind dread of man and what he can do to us (Numbers 14:9). The fear of man is characterized by believing that another person has the ultimate power to impact our lives negatively, causing us to dread the damage they might do us. Proverbs 29:25-26 tells us that "Fear of man will prove to be a snare, but whoever trusts in the LORD is kept safe. Many seek an audience with a ruler, but it is from the LORD that man gets justice."

The fear of man puts us in a situation that is likely to lure us into trouble. If we are not careful, our trust will shift from God to man, and we will forget that God alone controls a king's actions and defends the cause of the poor and the just (Proverbs 29:26). Instead of trusting in God, we may fear our promotion board, heads of department, and so on, and by doing so allow man to usurp God's position in our lives, which is a form of idolatry.

According to Edward T. Welch, the fear of man can include peer pressure, people pleasing, and co-dependency. I personally agree with him because this fear can be subtle and go largely unnoticed. When we desire to please all of the people, all of the time, we can easily become overcommitted because we do not know how and when to say no. This is often a symptom that we are unwittingly battling against the fear of man. Perhaps we are forever worrying about other people's opinions of us. Those people, who are forever competing against each other, believing themselves to be successful, are probably living in the fear of man because their lives are still defined by other people rather than God. Paul, in 2 Corinthians 10:12, supports this point by admonishing us that, "We do not dare to classify or compare ourselves with some who commend themselves. When they measure themselves by themselves and compare themselves with themselves, they are not wise."

Some of us are afraid to share our faith in Christ with other people because of what they will think of us. Perhaps we suffer from the fear of man and forget about the repercussions of acting sinfully against the Lord. Fear of man can be triggered by a fear of punishment from our bosses, pastors, teachers, leaders, or any other figure of authority over us. While it is true that we should respect every authority, even our friends and especially our spouse, we should not allow anyone to take the place of God in our lives.

The fear of man reveals itself again when we are afraid of making mistakes or get easily embarrassed because the mistake we have made makes us look bad in other people's eyes. At other times the fear reveals itself when we are so constantly hungry for love that we either become too possessive or we allow others to exercise unhealthy control over us. We do these things out of a fear that the person may leave us or that someone outside will be able to steal them from us.

Jesus directly addressed the issue of the fear of man in the Gospel of Luke, when speaking to His disciples. He put it this way: "I tell you, my friends, do not be afraid of those who kill the body and after that can do no more. But I will show you whom you should fear: Fear him who, after the killing of the body, has power to throw you into hell. Yes, I tell you, fear him" (Luke 12:4-5).

Jesus had just finished addressing the Pharisees with the pronouncement of the six woes against them (Luke 11:37-53). Jesus recognized that the harsh words He had spoken against the leaders had left them even more determined to trap Him, and He could see through the brave posturing of His disciples. He knew they were frightened of what the Pharisees could do to them. It was in this context that He taught them about the fear of God. That is, to respect the Lord's authority, stand in awe of His majesty, and trust and obey Him. Jesus taught His disciples to fear God more than men, irrespective of the perceived might of men's power. He wanted them to know that God has the ultimate power of final judgment.

This should be an encouragement to those going through persecution or the threat of such in the future. When we need something from other people, some are very gracious and will offer their unconditional help. Others will seek to put us into bondage, controlling us and feeding upon our inadequacy. A situation like this can really get out of control, to the extent that we become uncomfortable about making any decision for ourselves without consulting the person to whom we have (perhaps unwittingly) given permission to have control over us. In this case we have allowed him or her to usurp the role of God in our lives. This person could be our father, mother, wife, husband, teacher, pastor, friend, or relative.

Instead of fearing other people and being in awe of man, we should lovingly respect people while reserving the highest esteem for God. Remember that God expects us to respect our parents and obey whatever authority is over us, irrespective of their religious persuasions. The only condition attached is that we are to politely say no if instructed to do things that are in direct contradiction to the Word of God. Also, we are to love, obey, and have mutual respect for our spouses, colleagues, brothers, and sisters. This chapter is not a license to disrespect and disobey our elders, pastors, managers, parents, or other authorities!

The Use of Fear in Ministry

The Apostle Paul provided ministers with a working manual that is useful for all of us: "For the appeal we make does not spring from error or impure motives, nor are we trying to trick you. On the contrary, we speak as men approved by God to be entrusted with the gospel. We are not trying to please men but God, who tests our hearts. You know we never used flattery, nor did we put on a mask to cover up greed—God is our witness. We were not looking for praise from men, not from you or anyone else" (1 Thessalonians 2:3-6)

This challenges us to check our motives for being in the ministry and for reaching out to help others. Our motive should be to glorify God and minister in obedience to His command. When we minister in accordance with God's will, real changes will be manifested in people's lives. These would not occur if we were motivated by greed or using flattery, trickery, and fear as weapons to manipulate people through spiritual witchcraft.

Likewise, ministering to please men or seek acceptance from men instead of God is an indication that our hearts are not right with God. Our desire must be to please Him at all times using the weapons of holiness, gentleness, and loving-kindness. If we fail in this endeavor, it is important that we do not allow past failures and man's opposition to stop us from repenting and changing our ways. Ministers are to be faithful to their calling, acting in the spirit of servanthood as Jesus taught, and being cautious of pride and self-elevation.

For the rest of us, Paul advises in 1 Corinthians 4:1-21 that we need to respect and give ministers of God due regard as our spiritual fathers in Christ. They are not to be overvalued because they are ministers of Christ. At the same time, their value is not to be underestimated because they are ministers of the divine Father and not stewards of the things of this world. Paul urges all believers to learn from the ministers of God so as not to go beyond the Word of God in our daily walk.

GIVE TO CAESAR WHAT BELONGS TO CAESAR

Jesus instructed us to "give to Caesar what is Caesar's, and to God what is God's" (Luke 20:25). We may not approve of every requirement of the civil government, but Christians are to respect the law of the land and give everyone their due honor.

However, we are to revere, adore, and fear God only. There is another obedience that Christians owe to God; that is obedience to the Scriptures. We should not allow the fear of temporal loss or displeasure to tempt us to do things that the Scriptures plainly forbid.

If *Caesar* (or our present-day authorities) were to introduce a new gospel, it would be wrong for us to obey it. Instead, we should hold fast like the three friends of Daniel who refused to serve king Nebuchadnezzar's idol. Like them, we may suffer temporary discomfort when persecuted for putting our faith in the saving hand of the Lord. But God did not disappoint Daniel's friends—they were rescued from the fire without any need for hospital treatment. You may read more about the tyrant king in Daniel 3. We, too, must give to God what is God's and let Him fulfill His covenant with us in return.

This subject is unquestionably one of great difficulty and delicacy. It is important that we should not attempt to wrestle away power from the Caesars of this world by force or out of our own selfish ambitions. Instead, Christians should constantly pray for the wisdom that comes from Heaven. James puts it like this: "But the wisdom that comes from heaven is the first of all pure; then peace-loving, considerate, submissive, full of mercy and good fruit, impartial and sincere" (James 3:17).

The Bible assures us that if our ways are pleasing to God and we are doing His will, our angry enemies will lie down confused and ashamed because He is our ever-present helper (Isaiah 41:13). Our sorrow and mourning will disappear, and we will be overcome with joy and gladness (Isaiah 35:10, Psalm 23:6). Instead of fearing man, we can face him with courage and confidence because we know man's limitations and are well aware that all men will ultimately answer to God (Psalm 27:1-3). Like King David, we need to let our security be rooted in the Lord; even when evil men advance and besiege us. We should meditate on God's promises of deliverance in the Psalms and receive divine courage, which comes from trusting, confessing, and believing in the saving hand of God.

And if our enemies prove to be worthy opponents and resist the counsel of God, we need to be assured that, while the strong man may harm our bodies, emotions, and feelings (soul), he cannot touch our spirit because it is sealed. It is only God who can destroy both the soul and body in hell, so we need only to fear Him (Matthew 10:28). Jesus looked Pontius Pilate in the face and was not afraid because He knew that man's power over Him was limited to that which is given by the Father in Heaven. God is the ultimate source of all power (John 19:8-11).

THE STORY OF BLACK BART

I read the story of a bandit called Black Bart, who paraded the town with a deadly weapon, terrorizing stage coach travelers without ever firing a shot. He enjoyed a long reign of terror depriving people not only of valuables, but also of peace and joy. He manipulated people with the fear of what he could do to them with his big gun and fed on people's vulnerability.

As a testimony to the saving grace of God, Black Bart turned out to be a mild-mannered pharmacist who was terrified of horses. He later explained that he never fired a shot because his gun was never loaded.

Like Black Bart, the enemy only wants to rob us of God's best for our lives, so he gives us *False Evidence Appearing Real* (FEAR). He uses such weapons as fear of the unknown, and taunts us about our failures and inactivity when waiting upon the Lord. Satan's strategy is to deny us of our heritage through the use of deceitful thoughts to trap us into disobeying the Lord's commands. In a negative way, Satan presents things that are not as if they were; and, when we believe him, we call God a liar and empower Satan to control our emotions with fear.

Believers, the next time Satan attempts to sow doubt and fear into your life, declare trust in the Lord as David did in Psalm 56:3-4: *"When I am afraid, I will trust in you. In God, whose word I praise, in God I trust; I will not be afraid. What can mortal man do to me?"*

David's attitude speaks of trust and total reliance on the delivering power of God in the face of trouble. We learn from him that we need to make a personal confession when man threatens us with his demi-god-like status. Man has no power over our souls. We need to declare with David, "The LORD is with me; I will not be afraid. What can man do to me? The LORD is with me; he is my helper. I will look in triumph on my enemies" (Psalm 118:6-7).

David was so confident in the saving power of the Lord that he continued his thanksgiving in Psalm 118:8-9 by asserting, "It is better to take refuge in the LORD than to trust in man. It is better to take refuge in the LORD than to trust in princes."

David had already tasted the goodness of God in his past battles; and, being a king himself, he knew the truth that no king is saved by the size of his army, and no warrior escapes by his own great strength (Psalm 33:16-18). He knew that it is the presence of God that makes the difference between success and failure, and he concluded that he would rather praise and revere the Lord than man. David was not disappointed, as we see him praising the Lord for answering his prayers in Psalm 34. The writer of Hebrews caught this same revelation and encourages us to say with confidence, "The Lord is my helper; I will not be afraid. What can man do to me?" (Hebrews 13:6).

Personal Experience

Just like Edward Welch, the author of *When People are BIG and God is Small*, I had always been shy and self-conscious. I always wanted to do right by everyone, willingly letting myself be controlled by people's opinions and following their advice, even if my better judgment was contrary to that advice. Believe me; I suffered immeasurable agony as a result. The turning point for me was when I heard my respected advisers turn around and say, "Am I God? Can't you think for yourself?"

I realized that man's opinion and advice had caused me untold suffering and that it was time to change. Man had become bigger than God in my life. It is good to listen to man's advice and appreciate people for caring about us, but we need to bring God into the equation by asking for His counsel. Perhaps I should have gone to God first and meditated on His Word to find answers to my situations. I also realized that I had to refuse to be moved by the threat of man and to focus instead on God's promises.

My problem with the fear of man was strongly manifested when I wanted to make a decision to follow Christ and begin a wonderful walk with Him. I went through emotional turmoil, afraid of what my devout Muslim father would say and worrying about the effects on my friends and family. I wondered if I was betraying my Islamic faith. However, Jesus stood at the door of my heart, knocking persistently. I eventually realized that I would be changing camp from darkness to light and that the only way to the heavenly Father was through confessing Jesus as my Lord and Savior. I was made to understand that Jesus loves me unconditionally, so much that He died for me while I was yet a sinner in order to give me the opportunity of living with Him eternally.

I am grateful to Jesus for His mercy and patience with me because He eventually worked through all that fear in me and by so doing delivered me from the spirit of Islam. I willingly confessed my sin and began a wonderful journey with Him. The fruit of this journey is the book you are reading today.

It was important for me to know and be fully persuaded that the moment I entered through the gate to eternal life in Jesus Christ, by believing in Him for the forgiveness of my sins, I dramatically altered my destiny. Jesus said, "I am the gate; whoever enters through me will be saved" (John 10:9).

I was once blind and destined for eternal separation from God, but can now see and am destined to spend eternity with God as His child in Heaven. After passing through the gate to life, God began to conform me "to the likeness of His Son" (Romans 8:29). His goal is that my sole desire be to bring Him glory and praise His name forever.

I am now aware that I do not have to measure up to man's standards and opinions, because God's opinion of me is the deciding factor. My identity now should be rooted in the finished work of Jesus on the Cross. I now recognize that Jesus loves me and that I am righteous in His sight. He is constantly saying to me, "This is my beloved Son, in whom I am well pleased" (Mark 1:11, KJV). His thoughts toward me are good and pure. I have access to all the blessings in Christ Jesus.

THE FEAR OF MAN IN OPERATION

As mentioned above, the fear of man can come from human intimidation through our bosses, teachers, leaders or any others who may choose to use fear as a means of control. Man's inner pull toward sin can exhibit itself in many ways, which may include oppression of the poor, envy, greed, insensitivity and unfulfilled vows. It may also include pride, anger, discontentment, foolish talk, and injustice to others.

When we see the exhibition of sin and our oppression of one another, we are often paralyzed by the thought of what man could do to us because of our failure or refusal to carry out certain orders that may have been against God's personal instruction to us.

Reverend Sameh Maurice, a pastor based in Egypt, made the following comment when asked to speak on the constant threats by the press to Christians in that region. He said, "The language of our city is to threaten. If you cannot be intimidated, you cannot be threatened. We are fighting a spiritual battle—the spirit of hatred and fear versus the spirit of love." Praise God for that divine revelation! It also blessed my soul to read from the February, 2002, edition of *Charisma Magazine* about the bravery of some Egyptian Christians who refused to give in to threats from the state security intelligence police and Islamic fundamentalists. In spite of rejection and the reality of being ostracised by their families, they have simply refused to disown Jesus Christ. I believe God will honor them as they have honored Him. Amen!

SOME EXAMPLES OF THE FEAR OF MAN

My discussions with some people of Asian origin and Islamic background indicate that the fear of man is preventing a significant number of people from beginning a wonderful relationship with Jesus Christ. Such people generally fear the opinions and persecution that may come from their family members who are entrenched in worshiping a god that cannot save their soul.

Reading through the January, 2004, edition of the *Jews for Jesus* newsletter, the same enemy shows up. In this newsletter the story is told of a family who were searching for the meaning of life. They eventually met some people from the same background as themselves who were believers in Christ Jesus and shared their fears about what family members might say if they came to believe in Jesus for themselves.

The intimidation of the fear of man has so far prevented these people from knowing their Creator, but hope is not lost—God will have the final say in their situation.

Finally, I see the fear of man in cults that make their religious leader co-equal with Jesus Christ and frequently put fear into their follower's hearts. These cults say that your salvation will be lost if you leave them. They exalt their leaders above Christ. The attitude of those leaders is no other than predatory, and their beliefs are centerd upon a man who is trying to gain power, money, or influence by manipulating people. Many cults perpetuate dependency to the extent that followers lose the ability to make independent, rational decisions. They often use the technique of brainwashing to create robot-like behavior. This cult behavior has nothing to do with the fear of God but is strongly related to the fear of man, which will prove to be a snare (Proverbs 29:25).

Examples from the Bible

1 Samuel 17:11-45

This is the familiar story of David and Goliath. Saul and all the Israelite soldiers were dismayed and terrified at the appearance of Goliath, who tormented them every day. They all ran from him in great fear. When everyone saw Goliath as too big to kill, David was filled with holy anger and asked, "Who is this uncircumcised Philistine that he should defy the armies of the living God?" (verse 26).

David's confidence in the Lord enabled him to declare in verse 45, "You come against me with sword and spear and javelin, but I come against you in the name of the LORD Almighty, the God of the armies of Israel, whom you have defied."

We all know the result of that contest. David won and killed Goliath with a single stone. The battle is truly of the Lord!

Daniel 3:1-28

The story of Daniel's friends in Daniel 3:17-18 tells us that it is better to obey God than man. Shadrach, Meshach, and Abednego refused to serve King Nebuchadnezzar's idol and were thrown into the blazing furnace because they had implicit faith in the saving hand of their God. They put it like this, "If we are thrown into the blazing furnace, the God we serve is able to save us from it, and he will rescue us from your hand, O king" (Daniel 3:17).

The three children of God respected the king's position of authority but affirmed the power of their God irrespective of the king's threat. They knew that nothing is impossible to the omnipotence of God; and He did not disappoint them. Nebuchadnezzar, through this experience, came to confess the supremacy of the Most High God. However, Nebuchadnezzar paid dearly for mistreating children of the Most High God as he was dethroned and sent into exile where he lived with wild animals until he renounced his sins. Just like King Nebuchadnezzar, sinners today are called to repent and acknowledge God so that He may restore us. Nebuchadnezzar was restored and became even greater than before.

First Peter 3:14 says, "But even if you should suffer for what is right, you are blessed. 'Do not fear what they fear ; do not be frightened.'"

This verse tells us that if we suffer for the sake of righteousness, we are blessed and should not fear man's intimidation. What a mighty God we serve!

2 Kings 5:1-14

This is the story of a great general of Aram called Naaman and the prophet Elisha. Naaman was so powerful, yet he had a socially unacceptable disease. The king of Aram could not help him, and in search of a cure Naaman decided to heed his servant's advice to seek out the Prophet Elisha. The great soldier's pride would have prevented him from receiving a cure, had it not been for his loyal servant who came to the rescue. Naaman finally submitted to the prophet and received his healing because he obeyed the Word of God.

In this story we see the struggle between prophetic versus secular power. What the King of Aram was powerless to do, Elisha accomplished. This is because Elisha was connected to a higher realm, to the King of all kings, who seeks to enable, not coerce. This story tells us that man's power is finite while God's power is infinite.

SOME ANTIDOTES TO THE FEAR OF MAN

The true meaning of man's creation is to be found in what is given to him in Christ. We cannot know the real man until we know him in and through Christ. Man grows more into God's image as he reflects back to God His glory in gratitude and faith.

Fear of man is one of the barriers to coming to God, hearing from Him, and doing His will. When we fear people, we are putting them above God. This is simply idolatry.

Proverbs 14:27 admonishes us to fear the Lord because fear of the Lord is a life-giving fountain that offers us escape from the snares of death.

According to Job 24:20, the wicked are exalted for a little while but are gone and brought low in the next moment, cut off as the tops of the ears of corn.

The psalmist said, "Do not fret because of evil men or be envious of those who do wrong; for like the grass they will soon wither, like green plants they will soon die away" (Psalm 37:1-2).

It is wickedness and spiritual witchcraft to put people under the bondage of fear. We have an assurance that the Lord will break the power of the wicked and uphold the righteous, whose future will be filled with peace (Psalm 37:35-37).

It is important to know that we are blessed if we suffer for the sake of righteousness, and that we need not fear intimidation by the world (1 Peter 3:14). Therefore, we have the assurance that God is on our side when we raise the standard of justice around us.

Dr. William Glasser says emotional turmoil and misery come from trying to control others through criticizing, complaining, punishing, blaming, bribing, and threatening. When we say to our daughters or sons, "If you marry that man, I will cut you off from my will," we are practicing control and manipulation, and the Lord hates this practice. Those who deny other people liberty or safety deserve neither liberty nor safety themselves. Those who deny people religious freedom are afraid of the effect of liberty. *Repent and get right with God!*

It is better to obey God than man. The three children of God told Nebuchadnezzar, "Our God whom we serve is able to deliver us from the burning fiery furnace, and he will deliver us out of thine hand, O king. But if not, be it known unto thee, O king, that we will not serve thy gods, nor worship the golden image which thou hast set up" (Daniel 3:17-18, KJV).

This was a true confession of their perfect faith, as they knew nothing to be impossible to the omnipotent God and affirmed themselves to stand in His mercy. They offered unto God the most humble obedience to be delivered at His good pleasure and will. They were not disappointed.

Fellowmen, made in the image and likeness of God, it is worth noting that the most radical remedy for the fear of man is the fear of the Lord. Instead of needing people more, we should aim to love them more and allow love to crowd out all our fears. When we stop seeking to manipulate others, we will begin to seek God's counsel regarding other people, and the spirit and power of love will gradually develop in our heart.

People of God, we need to remember that relationship is very important to our Father; that is why He spoke everything into existence except for man. God formed us as a sculptor moulds clay because He desires to have a relationship with us. He therefore expects us to have a good relationship with one another, even when others are selfish or behave badly (Christians or not). If we do this, there is no need to fear our brethren or constantly watch our backs against unexpected daggers. The light that shines out from us will eventually consume any darkness (Matthew 5:44-48, Matthew 5:10-12).

The Bible tells us there is no fear in love but perfect love casts out all fears. It is the heart of God that drives true believers into action. They have the heart of Jesus who healed the ten lepers without pre-requisites. In the face of challenges, hardships, disappointments, ridicule, and torment, true believers will not turn their backs on people. Instead, they will get up in the night and pray like Jesus, "Forgive them, for they do not know what they are doing" (Luke 23:34)

Let us trust in the Lord with all our hearts and not be afraid of men. The Bible says, "If God is for us, who can be against us?" (Romans 8:31). God is faithful and He loves us unconditionally. People have a number of conditions that dictate their love or respect for one another; but God has already decided to let mercy triumph over justice through the finished work of Christ. *Why not make a decision today to let mercy, forgiveness, and love triumph over the spirit of fear?*

Allowing love to triumph over fear can be painful. It can hurt to strip away layers of pride and crawl out from under the dominion of our old sinful nature to be conformed into the likeness of Jesus. But as we persevere and catch a glimpse of His glory, we will never again desire to be away from His presence.

In his book *When People Are Big and God Is Small*, Edward T. Welch gives three basic reasons why we fear other people. These are:

1. Because they can expose and humiliate us
2. Because they can reject, ridicule, or despise us
3. Because they can attack, oppress, or threaten us

He concludes that one common denominator in the three reasons above is the belief that people are bigger (that is more powerful and significant) than God. Out of the fear that creates in us, we then bow to other people, giving them the power and right to tell us what to feel, think, and do.

Moses was afraid of Pharaoh when God called him to go back to Egypt. He gave every excuse in the book, but God was determined to use him for His glory. The Lord said to him, "'Who gave man his mouth? Who makes him deaf or mute? Who gives him sight or makes him blind? Is it not I, the LORD? Now go; I will help you speak and will teach you what to say.' But Moses said, 'O Lord, please send someone else to do it.' Then the Lord's anger burned against Moses" (Exodus 4:11-14).

People of God, please do not leave it to someone else to speak the Word. Do not fear; only obey and deliver the message given to you by Him, and watch Him do His part. He was true to His word for Moses. He is longing to do the same thing for us if only we will minister in love and obey His direction. We need not use the big whip of fear to coerce people into doing God's will.

In Isaiah 57:11-12, the prophet spoke firmly against the Jews because they were destitute of the fear of God, though they boasted of their holiness and empty religion. Isaiah called them hypocrites who flattered themselves in their superstition. They acted haughtily and insolently toward God and men. Isaiah declares that the true fear of God cannot exist where the worship is not pure and consistent with His Word. In verses 12 and 13 the prophet then affirms that the Lord will no longer endure what He formerly endured, and that the people must turn back from their wicked deeds and unrighteous ways in order to enter into a full relationship with Him. The fear of God is the antidote to the fear of man.

OVERCOMING THE FEAR OF MAN

Edward T. Welch encourages us to take the following steps to be free from the fear of man:
• Understand and grow in the fear of the Lord because the person who fears God will fear nothing else.

• Ask God to shed His light on you and examine where your desires have been too big. When we locate this area of our lives, we find that God is small in that area and our desires have become big.

• Rejoice and enter into the finished work of Jesus, for He took away our shame, protected us from danger, accepted us, and filled us with His love.

• Need other people less and love other people more. Allow perfect love to cast out all fears.

• Seek, draw near, and submit to God's counsel.

In the next chapter we will explore more about this fear of God.

Bible Verses To Help Us

1. "And God said, Let us make man in our image, after our likeness: and let them have dominion over the fish of the sea, and over the fowl of the air, and over the cattle, and over all the earth, and over every creeping thing that creepeth upon the earth" (Genesis 1:26, KJV).
2. "What is man that you make so much of him, that you give him so much attention" (Job 7:17-21)?
3. "I tell you, my friends, do not be afraid of those who kill the body and after that can do no more. But I will show you whom you should fear: Fear him who, after the killing of the body, has power to throw you into hell. Yes, I tell you, fear him" (Luke 12:4-5).
4. "When I am afraid, I will trust in you. In God, whose word I praise, in God I trust; I will not be afraid. What can mortal man do to me" (Psalm 56:3-4)?
5. "The LORD is with me; I will not be afraid. What can man do to me? The LORD is with me; he is my helper. I will look in triumph on my enemies" (Psalm 118:6).
6. "It is better to take refuge in the LORD than to trust in man. It is better to take refuge in the LORD than to trust in princes" (Psalm 118:8-9).
7. "Give to Caesar what is Caesar's, and to God what is God's" (Luke 20:25).

8. "But the wisdom that comes from heaven is first of all pure; then peace-loving, considerate, submissive, full of mercy and good fruit, impartial and sincere" (James 3:17).

9. "You come against me with sword and spear and javelin, but I come against you in the name of the LORD Almighty, the God of the armies of Israel, whom you have defied" (1 Samuel 17:45).

10. "Our God whom we serve is able to deliver us from the burning fiery furnace, and he will deliver us out of thine hand, O king. But if not, be it known unto thee, O king, that we will not serve thy gods nor worship the golden image which thou hast set up" (Daniel 3:17-18, KJV).

11. "'Who gave man his mouth? Who makes him deaf or mute? Who gives him sight or makes him blind? Is it not I, the LORD? Now go; I will help you speak and will teach you what to say.' But Moses said, 'O Lord, please send someone else to do it.' Then the LORD'S anger burned against Moses" (Exodus 4:11-14).

12. "Who shall separate us from the love of Christ? Shall trouble or hardship or persecution or famine or nakedness or danger or sword? ... No, in all these things we are more than conquerors through him who loved us. For I am convinced that neither death nor life, neither angels nor demons, neither the present nor the future, nor any powers, neither height nor depth, nor anything else in all creation, will be able to separate us from the love of God that is in Christ Jesus our Lord" (Romans 8:35, 37-39).

13. "Blessed are those who are persecuted because of righteousness, for theirs is the kingdom of heaven. Blessed are you when people insult you, persecute you and falsely say all kinds of evil against you because of me. Rejoice and be glad, because great is your reward in heaven" (Matthew 5:10-12).

14. "Cursed is the one who trusts in man, who depends on flesh for his strength and whose heart turns away from the LORD. He will be like a bush in the wastelands; he will not see prosperity when it comes. He will dwell in the parched places of the desert, in a salt land where no one lives" (Jeremiah 17:5-6).

15. "Blessed is the man who trusts in the LORD, whose confidence is in him. He will be like a tree planted by the water that sends out its roots by the stream. It does not fear when heat comes; its leaves are

always green. It has no worries in a year of drought and never fails to bear fruit" (Jeremiah 17:7-8).

16. "Many seek the ruler's favour, but every man's judgment cometh from the LORD" (Proverbs 29:26, KJV).

17. "The fear of man bringeth a snare: but whoso putteth his trust in the LORD shall be safe" (Proverbs 29:25, KJV).

18. "Arise, O LORD, let not man triumph; let the nations be judged in your presence. Strike them with terror, O LORD; let the nations know they are but men" (Psalm 9:19-20).

19. "I, even I, am he who comforts you. Who are you that you fear mortal men, the sons of men, who are but grass, that you forget the LORD your Maker, who stretched out the heavens and laid the foundations of the earth, that you live in constant terror every day because of the wrath of the oppressor, who is bent on destruction? For where is the wrath of the oppressor" (Isaiah 51:12-13)?

NINE

FEAR OF THE LORD

We obey our earthly fathers, teachers, and those in authority, not always because of our love for them but because we fear their punishment. Some of us obey God for the same reason. In the context of this chapter, the fear of God refers to an awesome respect and devotion growing out of the greatness and power of God. To fear the Lord means to love, trust, and obey His commands—to do good and reject evil.

Those who live in obedience to the Lord receive a spirit of boldness in prayer and are free from doubt and fears. Among the many expressions in the Bible used for worshiping God there are some metaphors pertaining to fear. "Those who feared the LORD" is used as an expression for those who faithfully follow the Lord and obey His teachings (Malachi 3:16).

Those who fear God order their lives in accordance with His will. Psalm 128 promises those who fear the Lord and walk in His ways a blessed assurance of continuous generational blessing and security. The same promise awaits those churches that corporately fear and walk in the Lord's ways. Corporate anointing and blessing will pursue and overtake them. It will flow from the pastor or minister to the congregation (including children). Fruitfulness is their portion, and there will be no spiritual barrenness. All their inadequacy will diminish because they honor Him.

The people who fear the Lord must love and revere Him. They are filled with awe—that is, they have admiration, respect, and an overwhelming sense of reverential fear, wonder, and amazement of the divine. I was filled with awe when I read in Genesis 1, for the first time, that God created Heaven and earth in six days by speaking the words, "Let there be ..." (KJV). My youthful mind could not comprehend the fact that a creative God spoke this planet earth into existence.

Fear of the Lord is the only fear that removes all others. There is no other overwhelming fear of the Lord, especially when this is inspired in the revelation of the creative God. The Word of God says, "A son honoureth his father, and a servant his master: if then I be a Father, where is mine honour? And if I be a master, where is my fear" (Malachi 1:6, KJV)?

Are you a child of God? If so, where is the fear of the Lord in your heart? Where is the respect that is due to the Lord?

Who Is This God?

The purpose of this chapter is to reinforce the freedom that Christians have in Christ, to outline the beliefs of a selection of popular religious practices today, and also to help Christians understand the basics about their teachings so that we may share our faith more effectively with other people. It is important to know that what you read below is not intended to be all you need to know about these religious practices and as such cannot provide all the answers to your questions.

I must also emphasize that Christianity is a relationship with a loving Father and not a religion. The comparison drawn below is just to help readers who are searching for the truth to discover the real God and forsake all counterfeits. Friends, wouldn't you rather have authentic £20 or $20 notes than a truckload of worthless counterfeits? I have made my choice. What about you? Authentic or counterfeit? Choose authentic, and you will have life.

We have been talking about the reverence, respect, and fear of the Lord. But some readers may be asking the question: "Who is this God?" This is probably one of the oldest questions ever asked by mankind, and it certainly demands an answer if we are to fear Him and obey His commands. Some think of God as being like an old man who sits in Heaven looking at a crystal ball and holding a divine rod in His hand, watching to see if anyone will break His law. Others believe in a multitude of gods, ranging from Shiva to Buddha. Below is a short summary of some of the manmade gods people worship today.

Hinduism

The divine being in Hinduism is impersonal, while Christians serve a personal God with whom we have a daily relationship. Hindus worship countless deities and statues as well as a triune god called Trimurti, meaning "god in three forms". But in Christianity there is only one God, eternally existing and manifesting himself to us in three Persons known to man as Father, Son, and Holy Spirit, which are three separate personalities.

Hindu mythology is based on teachings about *karma*. Karma is the value of good and bad deeds undertaken in this life, which then affect what happens to a person in the next life. Among other things, Hinduism teaches that the universe is not the creation of a personal God but something that spreads out naturally from the divine, and as such has no beginning or end. Karma revolves around the belief that all living entities are caught in a cycle of birth, death, and rebirth, a process called *samsara*.

The Bible tells us in Genesis that the universe was created in six days by a creative God, who spoke everything into being. When Christians die, we simply relocate to Heaven to be with the Father for eternity; there are no cycles of birth, death, and rebirth. The new birth in Christianity occurs at the point of salvation, which is when you make a decision to make Jesus your Lord and Savior.

Hinduism solves the problem of suffering by referring to it as the deserving consequences of past deeds. Hindus believe that evil deeds carried out in this life will be repaid in the form of suffering in future lives. Performance of religious deeds, rituals, pilgrimages, and charitable giving are some of their ways of breaking the cycle of birth and death—in other words it is their way to salvation. As Christians, we know that religious activities and rituals cannot save anyone on their own; we are saved through our faith in Jesus.

The fate or status of a person in the Hindu religion is determined by the amount of good works he or she has accumulated during a previous existence. According to followers of Hinduism, the goal of any religious exercise is to find a way of escape from the endless cycle of birth and rebirth. The principle of karma is simply based on cause and effect of individual deeds, which are alien to the concepts of salvation, grace, forgiveness of sins, and a personal relationship with Jesus Christ.

Followers of Hinduism and other modern-day religions use weapons of fear, religious works, and every tactic necessary to keep their followers in spiritual bondage. These religions speak about love but are devoid of the love of the God who sacrificed His only Son to set every human being free.

Buddhism

Buddhism developed out of Hinduism around 500 B.C. Siddhartha Guatama named himself Buddha, meaning "The enlightened one," because of his discoveries concerning the path of enlightenment. Followers of this religion do not worship gods or deities. They believe that the pathway to enlightenment is found by personal spiritual development rather than by relying on outside support from God. History tells us that the founder of Buddhism was confronted with old age, illness, and possible death—a situation that made him renounce a life of supreme luxury to cultivate what he called "holy living," which centered upon a path of meditation, severe fasting, and self-discipline. However, a life of strict self-discipline and the avoidance of all pleasures and luxuries are of no use in gaining spiritual freedom. Religious works and self-reliance cannot save anyone. Salvation is only received by professing Jesus as Lord and Savior.

According to the award-winning religious diversity training book by Diversiton (see www.diversiton.com) a Buddhist believes, among other things, that human existence is painful and that death does not bring an end to suffering because of the cycle of death and birth. Selfish cravings and attachments are therefore the cause of our suffering; and the path toward the cessation of craving and attachment is an eight-fold path. The eight points are:
- right understanding,
- right purpose,
- right speech,
- right conduct,
- right livelihood,

- right effort,
- right alertness, and
- right concentration.

All this amounts to human wisdom, which cannot save anyone from the impending divine judgment awaiting all those who do not accept Jesus as Lord and Savior.

Buddhism sees ignorance rather than sin as the obstacle to salvation. The belief that the world and the self truly exist keeps their illusory wheel of existence rolling. In their eyes, only the destruction of that belief will stop the mad course of the world.

The goal of all existence in Buddhism is *nirvana*—reaching the gate of eternity. This is a state of non-existence in which all human attachments that cause suffering are cut off and cease to exist. In this state there is a complete cessation of both desire and personality. As mentioned above, the goal of Christianity is a loving relationship with God on earth and throughout eternity with the Father in Heaven.

Buddhists claim to achieve salvation by means of meditation, which is a continuous practice of the eight-fold path mentioned above and which is supposed to lead to the extinction of suffering. The life without Christ is a wasteful one, and it is destined for divine judgment in hell.

Judaism

The word Judaism comes from the Hebrew word *Yehudah*, meaning 'The Praised'. This religion is linked by three elements: the union of a God, a people (Israel), and a country (the Holy Land). The Torah (the five books of Moses) begins the Hebrew and Christian Bible.

The Jews believe in the Old Testament of the Bible. According to the biblical account in the Book of Exodus, the Children of Israel assembled at the wilderness of Sinai in the third month after they had gone out of Egypt. At this point, Moses went up to God, and the Lord instructed him to consecrate the people in readiness for the visitation from Him on the third day.

The people stood at the foot of the mountain while Moses went up to the Lord to receive the commands of the Lord popularly known as the Ten Commandments (Exodus 20:1-17).

These commandments are very authoritative and represents the heart of the Law in the Jewish tradition. The Jews believe that suffering is a mystery but that somehow God is Lord even in the midst of a painful and evil world.

To the followers of Judaism, God is a person—one with a different type of emotions to mankind but who desires to have a relationship with the people.

The Torah is the Jewish guide to correct living, and studying it is seen as a form of worship. Group prayer is very important, the time of which varies depending on the hour of the day, the day of the month, and the branch of Judaism. God is seen as active in a creative way, constantly working in the world to offer men help to fulfil their obligations toward Him and toward their fellowmen. Jews do not believe in Jesus as Lord; rather they see Him as a good teacher who performed great miracles.

Judaism says that one's eternal existence in the hereafter is determined by his moral behavior and attitudes. God always offers even the most evil of men the chance of repentance (*teshuva*, or turning). However the notions of individual salvation and heavenly existence are not prominent in Judaism. In fact many Jews criticize Christianity for being a selfish religion, too concerned with personal eternal rewards. Jews still hope for the coming of the Messiah, who will judge and reward all according to their deeds.

There are various branches of modern Judaism, ranging from Orthodox to Conservative to the Reformed Jews. The approach to spirituality also varies from the radical to monotheistic. The most important difference between Judaism and Christianity is that followers of Judaism reject Jesus' claims to be the Messiah and Deliverer, thus fulfilling the saying of Jesus, "No prophet is accepted in his home town" (Luke 4:24).

Islam

The word *Islam* means the act of submission and resignation of oneself. One who professes Islam is a Muslim—one who has submitted to Allah as revealed through the message and life of his prophet, Muhammad. Allah, which means *God* in Arabic, is the god of Islam, a religion founded by Muhammad about 600 A.D. on a strict monotheistic (one god) basis that spread throughout the Middle East region through the use of military conquest.

The followers of Allah accept Jesus Christ as being a prophet (Prophet Issa) but reject the Trinity and the divinity of Christ (Q5:73). Muslims accept that Jesus was sent by God the Father with the gospel (Q5:46) and recognize His birth from a virgin (Q3:45-47). They also believe in the miracles that He performed with the permission of the Father (Q5:110; 19:30-33). In fact, Jesus is popularly known in some Muslim circles as "the Miracle Worker."

Muslims do not believe that God would condescend to become a man and find the truth of God coming down to earth as a man very offensive (Q5:17, 75; 9:30). The *Quran* puts it like this: "Say, He is Allah, the One, Allah, the Eternal, Absolute; He begetteth not, nor is He begotten; and there is none like unto Him" (Q112:1-4). The Bible tells us about the affirmation of Jesus by the Father at the point of His baptism—"This is my beloved Son, in whom I am well pleased" (Matthew 3:17, KJV). They do not believe that Jesus was crucified on the Cross or that He died and was buried and rose in the body with His wounds intact on the third day (Q4:157).

Allah is personal to the Muslims, and he has no subordinate deities. There is an absolute prohibition of idols and any other means of representing God. Allah is also merciful and compassionate, but his mercy is shown in sending messengers to proclaim the truth. The goal of Islam is to make a moral order in the world. Conscience is the greatest value in Islam, much as love is the greatest value in Christianity.

At about the age of forty, Muhammad began to retire frequently for meditation to a cave on the slopes of Mount Hirah. During these periods of meditation, he seemed at times to be in a kind of trance where he claimed to have heard the voice of Allah or of the Archangel Gabriel. History has it that Allah communicated the word of God to Prophet Muhammad through the Angel Gabriel over a period of twenty-two years. These recitals are now known as the *Quran*, the Muslim Holy Scriptures. Muslims memorize and recite the *Quran* in Arabic, as it is thought to be authoritative only in that language. It is made up of 114 chapters (*suras*) and 6,000 verses.

The *Quran* teaches Muslims to spread Allah's message and to help the poor. It clearly and strongly states, that "there be no compulsion in religion" (Q2:256).

Some Muslims do not expect miraculous deliverance from suffering in this life but believe that good deeds will be rewarded in the next life. Like the Bible, the *Quran* states that the day of judgment will be preceded by clear signs and natural catastrophes, the appearance of the Anti-Christ (*Dajjad*), commotion in heaven and earth (Q101:1-5; 70:9-10), the darkening of the sun and moon (Q75:7-8; 81:1), and the event of the sudden second coming of Christ.

Islamic teachings come from both the *Quran* and the Hadith. The Hadith is a collection of traditions recording the words and deeds of Muhammad. Where the *Quran* and traditions are silent on a particular subject, rules are derived by consensus of the religious leaders (*ijma*) and by comparable reasoning (*qiyas*).

The Islamic law known as *Shariah* is a combination of the *Quran*, Hadith, the consensus of the religious leaders, and popular reasoning. Shariah law supports the use of draconian punishments for certain crimes, such as amputation for theft, stoning for adultery, and the death sentence for any Muslim who converts to Christianity. Some of the provisions of Shariah law infringe on human rights; for example, women are of less value than Muslim men. Shariah law also cancels out the freedom to choose one's own faith.

The *Quran* rejects the notion of redemption. And to the followers of Islam, salvation depends on a man's actions and attitudes. That is, repentance can quickly turn an evil man toward the virtue that will save him. Salvation through the work of God is alien to Muslims, the goal of whose existence work toward being in a sensual paradise with Allah. Muslims have to win Allah's good pleasure, and His good pleasure is everything to them (Q5:119; 25:15). In Islam, the biblical teachings of salvation in this life through faith in Jesus Christ are rejected, and freedom through the finished work of Jesus Christ on the Cross is also dismissed.

The five pillars of Islam are:

• Confessing the faith (*Shahada*)—"Testify that there is no god but Allah."

- Prayer (*Salah*)—five times a day with ablutions (washing of hands, face, legs, and head)
- Fasting (*Sawm*)—practised during the Ramadan period, but the exact time varies from one year to another
- Giving of alms—helps toward gaining more points on the judgment day
- Pilgrimage to Mecca—There is a requirement for Muslims to make at least one visit to the Islamic holy land in a lifetime.
- Some Muslims add Jihad, holy war, as a sixth pillar, but it is a man-made rule.

The *Quran* does not argue the existence of God. It simply assumes that Allah is. The *Kalima* (Muslim confession) states, "There is no deity but Allah" (*La ilah ill Allahu*). However, there are a number of people who live as Muslims though they are really Christians. They believe that Jesus (*Issa*) is the Master of heaven and earth but cannot openly proclaim Him as Lord for fear of prosecution.

Christianity—A Loving Personal Relationship with Christ

Christianity is unique in the sense that it claims God can be known as a personal God through His self-revelation in the Bible. The Bible was written not to prove the existence of God, but to reveal His character. The God of the Bible transcends all His creation because He is the Creator. Christianity is the only faith that claims its Founder came to earth as God in the flesh. Jesus came to show us what God is like in the only way we could fully understand—through human life. Other religions are unable to make this same claim concerning their gods. There is no Christianity without Jesus.

Those who dedicate their lives to the teaching of the Good News (the gospel) and works of Jesus Christ are called Christians. Acts 11:26 tells us that, "So for a whole year Barnabas and Saul met with the church and taught great numbers of people. The disciples were called Christians first at Antioch."

In Acts 26:28, Agrippa used *Christian* sarcastically; others used it to distinguish the Christian group from Judaism. The term "Christians," whether adopted by believers or invented by the world as a term of reproach, is an appropriate title for those belonging to Christ and is a comforting sign of God's glory (1 Peter 4:14-16).

Christians believe that Jesus was born on this earth nearly 2,000 years ago. He is the Son of the living God, who created the Heaven and the earth (Genesis 1:1). This same God created man in His own image and likeness (Genesis 1:26) and gave him life by breathing into his nostrils (Genesis 2:7). As the Son of God, Jesus came into the world, lived among us, was crucified, died and was buried, but rose again from the dead. Those who have faith in Jesus, His death, and resurrection can enter into a right relationship with God, for He and the Father are one. If Jesus did not pay for our sin when He died, then we are still unforgiven and Christianity is an empty promise of new life.

God is one, and there is no other God than Him. No one has seen God, except those who saw Him in a form He took upon himself temporarily for the occasion. Christ, the only begotten Son has made Him known to mankind (John 1:18). If anyone acknowledges that Jesus is the Son of God, God lives in him and he in God (1 John 4:15).

Though God is one, there are three persons in the one Godhead (the Father, the Son, and the Holy Spirit). The Bible tells us in Matthew 3:16-17 that the moment Jesus came out of the baptism water the Holy Spirit of God came upon Him to affirm and equip Him for His work, and the voice of the Father said, "This is my beloved Son, in whom I am well pleased" (Matthew 3:17, KJV).

As the Father, God is infinite in love, power, and wisdom. Jesus, the Son, was incarnated in order to reveal God to humankind. The Holy Spirit is another manifestation of God. The ministry of the Holy Spirit is to testify that Jesus is the Son of God and a personal Savior for all mankind. It is also His ministries to dwell in believers' hearts, empower us, and convict those who have not yet started a personal relationship with God.

God is therefore a Spirit, and those that worship Him must worship Him in Spirit and in truth (John 4:24). God is without a physical body or form (except when revealed as the Son). He is invisible. It is the ministry of the Holy Spirit to enable people to grow in the understanding and concept of God as Spirit.

Christians communicate with God through worship, prayer, and meditating on God's Word (the Bible). The Bible (made up of the Old and New Testaments) is to be regarded as the authoritative Word of truth on all matters of basic doctrine: "The grass withers and the flowers fall, but the word of our God stands forever" (Isaiah 40:8).

The Bible is inspired by God and was given to mankind for the purpose of teaching, reproof, correction, and training in righteousness so that we may be adequately equipped for every good work (2 Timothy 3:16-17).

Christians believe that everything God created (including man) was good and that the present state of this world is due to the sin committed by the first couple that were created (Adam and Eve). Man was created to have a personal relationship with God, but sin has severed that spiritual relationship with Him. We are now all born with a nature of sin because of the sin committed by Adam and Eve. We are therefore inherently sinful from our mother's womb, which is the reason for all the evil that exists in the world. The consequence of sin is spiritual death, and the gift of God is eternal life (Romans 6:23). The Lord loved the world so much that He gave us His only Son (Jesus) to pay the penalty for our sin. He is the only perfect one capable of paying the price for the penalty we ultimately deserve, which is death. For it is impossible for the blood of bulls and goats to take away sins (Hebrews 10:4).

Christians believe that we cannot save ourselves and make ourselves perfect and thus acceptable to God, try as we may. The Bible puts it this way: "And there is salvation in no one else; for there is no other name under heaven that has been given among men, by which we must be saved" (Acts 4:12, NASV).

That is the reason Jesus was able to declare without any reservation, "I am the way and the truth and the life. No one comes to the Father except through me" (John 14:6).

It is the will of God that every man should be saved, so anyone who believes in Him will not perish but have eternal life (John 3:16) "For it is by grace you have been saved, through faith—and this not from yourselves, it is the gift of God—not by works, so that no one can boast" (Ephesians 2:8-9). "Christ is the end of the law so that there may be righteousness for everyone who believes" (Romans 10:4).

Salvation only comes from a saving faith in Christ Jesus. He is calling everyone to repent because there is an appointed time for judging the world in righteousness through a Man whom He has appointed, having furnished proof to all men by raising Him from the dead (Acts 17:31). The purpose of faith in Christ is not primarily religion but relationship—to know God personally and enjoy intimate and uninterrupted communion with Him forever.

In his book *But Don't All Religions Lead to God?*, Michael Green likens the search for God to people trying to find their way through a maze. There are lots of routes that bring us to a dead end and fail to get us out of the maze. He concludes by saying there is just one way through. That way is through Jesus, who said in John 10:9, "I am the gate; whoever enters through me will be saved. He will come in and go out, and find pasture. The thief comes only to steal and kill and destroy; I have come that they may have life, and have it to the full."

That is a glorious promise. He has come to move us from a position of defeat to one of victory. Praise God! He is the only way to salvation, and His purpose is to give us abundant life.

We cannot say the same of the thief (Satan), whose goal is to steal, kill, and destroy God's people. In his book *Question of Life*, Nicky Gumbel says, "Life without a relationship with God through Jesus Christ is like the television without the aerial." This is profound because life without a relationship with God through Jesus Christ is devoid of clarity and ultimately meaningless. There is something better than what you are experiencing today. It is a life with clarity, purpose, and abundance that is not limited to this world but is eternal, and which transfers ultimately to the presence of God in Heaven.

Jesus offers clarity and not arrogant elitism. He offers solid ground to stand on in the midst of the dangerous varieties of human religious opinion. The Bible calls the Church the Bride of Christ. To complete the joining together of husband and wife, each person has to say "I do." Likewise each individual must say "I do" to Jesus, followed by "I don't" to all other suitors.

[If you are reading this and have not repented from your wicked ways and want to know how to escape this eternal judgment, you should go straight to Appendix 1, "The Decision," located at the back of this book, where you will find a sample of a personal template for renouncing sin and entering into a personal relationship with Jesus. To die without Christ is to be eternally separated from God.]

I feel the love of God for you and would encourage you to remove the barrier and allow God to come into your life. He is standing at the door of your heart, knocking and romancing you (Revelation 3:20). Will you allow Him to come in and eat with you?

To conclude this section I would like to quote from one of the Apostle Paul's writings in 1 Corinthians 8:5-7 (NASB): "For even if there are so-called gods whether in heaven or on earth, as indeed there are many gods and many lords, yet for us there is but one God, the Father, from whom are all things, and we exist for Him; and one Lord, Jesus Christ, by whom are all things, and we exist through Him. However not all men have this knowledge."

Paul recognized the obvious fact that there are many who are worshiped as gods and there are many myths being spread by many gurus, which lead people astray by enticing them with miracles and false promises. These so-called gods are false; they cannot save you and should not be attributed with divine status. An idol is nothing and possesses no power. The sacrifices of pagans are offered to demons and not to God. Christians are therefore warned not to become participants with demons by eating with pagans in their temple feasts (1 Corinthians 10:20).

I can declare unashamedly that the Lord I am talking about is the Creator of all existing things. "In the beginning God created the heavens and the earth" (Genesis 1:1).

He is the one that the Apostle John described as the Word in John 1:1-3: "In the beginning was the Word, and the Word was with God, and the Word was God."

He is the Judge, who judges us through His Word by His Spirit and by His perfect and holy nature; He is the Shepherd in John 10:11 which says, "I am the good shepherd. The good shepherd lays down his life for the sheep."

He is the same God that David referred to when he said, "The LORD is my shepherd, I shall not be in want" (Psalm 23:1).

He is the one who is infinite (1 Kings 8:27). He is omnipotent—He has all power and can do all things. He is omnipresent—that is He is present at all times in all parts of His creation and universe. He is the omniscient one—He has all knowledge and knows all things simultaneously. He is the changeless God: there is no variability in

Him, no shadow of turning (James 1:17). He is long-suffering toward sinful humans (Exodus 34:6) but capable of showing vengeance (Deuteronomy 32:35, Romans 12:19). He is love because love is His nature (1 John 4:8, 16). My God is eternal (Genesis 21:33, Deuteronomy 33:27, Jeremiah 10:10, 1 Timothy 1:17, Romans 16:26). His existence had no beginning (Isaiah 44:6-11) and will have no ending. He always was, always is, and always will be. He is the great "I Am Jehovah," who is unchangeable; the true living God (John 1:1-5, 1 Thessalonians 1:9, Jeremiah 10:10). "But the LORD is the true God, he is the living God, and an everlasting king: at his wrath the earth shall tremble, and the nations shall not be able to abide his indignation" (Jeremiah 10:10, KJV).

In addition to the above, He has revealed himself by many names in the Bible. The above is by no means an exhaustive list.

God is not like groceries that you need to choose from the supermarket shelf where a multitude of goodies scream at you, "Take me home." He speaks to you instead through His gentle Spirit, using the still, small voice of the Holy Spirit.

Some people peddle a variety of so-called gods and declare, "There is only one God, and all faiths lead to the same God." Others say, "I like Buddha, you like Jesus. It doesn't really make any difference." I say it is untrue. Just look at the nature of these gods that people are peddling. Most people are worshiping the created rather than the Creator. Can these gods create anything? Do they have anything compared to the nature of the God described above?

The prophet Isaiah made a wonderful presentation to the Jews who were worshiping idols. He asked the following: "To whom then will you liken God? Or what likeness will ye compare to Him? The workman melteth a graven image, and the goldsmith spreadeth it over with gold, and casteth silver chains. He that is so impoverished that he hath no oblation chooseth a tree that will not rot; he seeketh unto him a cunning workman to prepare a graven image, that shall not be moved. Have ye not known? have ye not heard? hath it not been told you from the beginning? have ye not understood from the foundations of the earth? It is he that sitteth upon the circle of the earth, and the inhabitants thereof are as grasshoppers; that stretcheth out the heavens as a curtain, and spreadeth them out as a tent to dwell in" (Isaiah 40:18-22, KJV).

I believe readers will agree with me that God is much bigger than our concept of Him allows. The Lord who created all things is all-powerful and the source of true wisdom. For readers who are still unsure of this God, I pray that He will give you a spirit of wisdom and revelation to know Him, that your eyes and heart will be opened to know the riches of the glory of Christ. Amen! (Ephesians 1:17-18).

Speaking through the prophets, He declares, "'To whom will you compare me? Or who is my equal?' says the Holy One" (Isaiah 40:25). It is very degrading when we compare Him with idols. *Who is God to you?*

THE WISDOM OF GOD

We have looked briefly at the fear of the Lord. Now let us check the meaning of wisdom. It is said that a wise man has the ability to make a right decision or judgment by applying intelligent thought to a wide range of experience and knowledge.[1]

What is wisdom? Wisdom is the body of knowledge and experience that develops within a specified society or period. It includes astuteness, common sense, discernment, insight, perceptiveness, prudence, and understanding. Wisdom is the knowledge of life and the ability to understand that the all-knowing God who created all things has designed a moral universe with consequences for every decision we make.

A man in Christ has the God-given ability to live rightly in accordance with God's command. Wisdom must begin with obedience and culminate in praise. It is the affirmation that all of life is best understood and most truly discerned in relation to God's governance and sovereignty. Proverbs 1-9 metaphorically personifies wisdom as a woman in a variety of positive female roles.

The female figures of wisdom first appear in Proverbs speaking as a prophet (Proverbs 1:20-33), a profession to which both men and women were called.

The Bible also likens wisdom to a high-ranking woman who can employ a messenger. In the Book of Proverbs, both the ideal wife

(31:10) and the woman wisdom (3:15; 8:11) are described as being more precious than jewels.

Proverbs 4:6 enjoins the listener not to forsake wisdom, as she will protect you. Proverbs 4:7 asserts that wisdom is supreme and as a result should rank first on our list of priorities. A person who uses the wisdom of the Lord in business dealings will be bestowed with riches and honor (Proverbs 8:18, 21).

Wisdom is a counselor and a teacher (Proverbs 8:6-10, 8:14); she is a life-giver and one of God's instruments to guide and guard mankind.

Proverbs 9:10 declares, "The fear of the LORD is the beginning of wisdom, and knowledge of the Holy One is understanding." This Scripture tells us that God is the source of wisdom and insight. And Psalm 111:10 puts it this way, "The fear of the LORD is the beginning of wisdom: a good understanding have all they that do his commandments: his praise endureth forever" (KJV).

This means you are on the road to embracing your friend (wisdom) when you acknowledge, revere, and submit to the only wise one. The result of acknowledging, revering, and submitting to God is that all other fear is put under His control. How do I know this? Psalm 34:7 tells us that "the angel of the LORD encamps around those who fear him, and he delivers them."

Fear not, for those who are with you are more than those who are against you. The fundamental principle of wisdom is a relationship of reverence and submission to the Lord.

When you recognize Him as Jehovah Nissi—the Lord Is Our Banner (Exodus 17:15)—you can boldly declare with the psalmist that the Lord is your fortress. He is the one who protects you from the deadly pestilence and drives away all fears, even though you see the evidence of pestilence and plague all around (Psalm 91). The Word of God will minister to your heart, and you will suddenly get a revelation that all the diseases of Egypt will not come near your dwelling place, and that everyone and everything concerning you is safe in His loving hand. That is the wisdom from above. Jesus teaches us to acknowledge the Lord before others. That is, to respect and revere the Lord in all our ways, which simply translates to fear of the Lord.

Wisdom in the fullest sense belongs to God alone. His wisdom is not only the completeness of knowledge pertaining to every realm of life, but also consists of the irresistible fulfilment of whatever He has in mind. The universe and man are the products of His creative wisdom. Natural and historic processes are governed by His wisdom, which includes infallible discrimination between good and evil.

Biblical wisdom is more than knowing facts and figures.[2] It transcends recollecting Scripture verses from memory and is greater than good judgment or taking the right course of action. It surpasses cleverness, as there are many clever people who are devoid of the wisdom of God. And it is certainly above accumulating philosophic, scientific, and theological knowledge. Biblical wisdom is both religious and practical. It stems from the fear of the Lord and branches out to touch all of life. It takes insights gleaned from the knowledge of God's ways and applies them to our daily walk. Wisdom builds a house, ministry, church, or business; it helps when counseling, during mediation, and makes you a good and respected leader. It eventually leads to success in all your undertakings. Wisdom is very crucial when ministering the Word of God, and especially when releasing the prophetic Word of God to His children. Failure to apply godly principles and wisdom may bring down an anointed man of God in ministry and may cause dissention within the house of God. Wisdom rewards those who combine insight, knowledge, and cordial love with obedience to God's instruction (Proverbs 9:12).

CONNECTION BETWEEN WISDOM AND THE FEAR OF THE LORD

The connection between wisdom and the fear of the Lord is highlighted in 1 Kings 3:3-28, where it is reported that, "Solomon showed his love for the LORD by walking according to the statutes of his father David, except that he offered sacrifices and burned incense on the high places" (1 Kings 3:3).

Solomon did as he was commanded and probably went beyond the call of duty. This tells us that Solomon feared the Lord and desired to obey His command. Solomon recognized his shortcomings, and when God presented a life-changing opportunity to him in a most famous dream, he wasted no time in requesting a good thing—wisdom from the Lord. This is what all true believers should desire instead of seeking the wisdom of the world.

Solomon could have asked for wealth, honor, power to destroy his enemies, long life, and more! But in great humility, he recognized that God had given him a big job and that only He could provide the necessary equipment for Solomon to execute his responsibilities well. So Solomon asked for wisdom. He wanted an understanding heart. He wanted to disseminate justice in line with God's command. He sought to do good and to shun evil. But he also recognized that human wisdom would not suffice, so he sought true wisdom from the Giver of all gifts.

We are told that Solomon's request pleased God so that He immediately granted the king's request. "Behold, have done according to thy words: lo, I have given thee a wise and an understanding heart; so that there was none like thee before thee, neither after thee shall any arise like unto thee" (1 Kings 3:12, KJV).

Since Solomon went beyond the call of duty earlier, God decided to go beyond the bounds of Solomon's request. God gave Solomon the gift of wisdom, and both riches and honor.

Solomon was patient, discerning, and attentive to the character and quality of his life. Simply put, Solomon feared God. From the above, we can safely infer that fear of the Lord leads to wisdom, and wisdom brings success, riches, and honor. He who does not fear the Lord denies himself of the Lord's wise counsel and all the benefits associated with wisdom.

Solomon focused on how to be a good king and requested the necessary anointing to function well as king. His main problem was how to serve God faithfully. He did not rely on his own understanding but allowed God to teach him the difference between good and evil. Solomon knew that real knowledge could only be found in the fear of the Lord. Through acquiring the fear of the Lord he also received understanding and divine wisdom.

Solomon was not cheated by anyone. Instead, he received things he had not asked for—houses full of all good things, which he himself did not fill (Deuteronomy 6:10-11). It takes the fear of God to make such a beginning in wisdom, because he who fears the Lord does not seek after many things but single-mindedly seeks after the one thing that is necessary. Solomon received all these blessing because he dared to fear God. Jesus put it this way, "But seek first the kingdom of God and His righteousness, and all these things shall be added to you" (Matthew 6:33, NKJV).

Psalm 49 delivers a chilling warning to those who are in awe of the rich, in order that they may be freed from this spell. The psalmist had observed the attitude of many rich people. Having seen their folly, he then offers his wisdom. He says that rich people proudly rely on their great wealth and personal ability to assure their security in the world.

Some rich people may think they are wise in their own eyes because they fail to recognize the Lord as the Giver of all gifts and the one who has given them the power to get wealth. This attitude is devoid of the fear of the Lord. Scripture says inescapable death is the destiny of those devoid of this fear and only God can redeem their lives from the grave (Psalm 49:13-15). However, there is good news in the midst of the prophecy of doom for the rich fools. They who turn their ears to the wisdom of God and obey His law will not perish. Even though they may sleep temporarily, they will be resurrected with the saints on the day of judgment. Our Lord is a merciful God, and He is interested in the salvation of all mankind, rich and poor alike. He is grieved when secularism, materialism, and disdain of the covenant ideals squeeze the fear of God from our lives.

At times, people can be so proud of their success that they wrongly assume they don't need God. Let's be clear that the earth belongs to God, and everything in all the world is His. He is the one who pushed the oceans back to let dry land appear (Psalm 24:1-2). That tells me that we owe all our wealth and successes—everything—to God. No matter how much a person achieves, without God, he or she eventually comes to nothing (Obadiah 1:3-4). A person will accomplish much more of lasting value living for Christ.

Personally, I have nothing against rich people because there are so many good rich people (Christians and non-Christians) who use their wealth to build the kingdom of God and who are regularly a blessing to the world around them. These people most likely have fear of the Lord in their hearts and recognize the Lord as the source of their wealth. One of my proofreaders pointed out to me that I should be careful how I analyze this topic because the Lord may shower me with the blessings of obedience from the publishing of this book, so that my house may not be enough to contain it! I say a resounding "Amen" to that prayer because I live to be a blessing to others on a daily basis; financial and spiritual blessings are my birthright.

However, God's perception of poverty is totally different from that of man. In God's eyes, we are poor only if we have no vision and no hope for the future. We are poor when our souls are unregenerate and our minds are filled with the filth of this sinful world. However, there is no poverty in a man who stands in Christ because he is joint heir to the infinite blessings and resources available through Christ Jesus. I must point out to any who believe Psalm 49 supports poverty in the Body of Christ that the Lord has nothing against the rich. He gives the rich the power to gain wealth. He is only against those who worship the rich or their wealth (and those who worship their own wealth). The Lord loves all mankind and reminds the rich that He is their source of blessing, and that as a result nothing and no one should be worshiped except Him.

The psalmist finally distinguishes between life in Christ and those who are devoid of God. A life without Christ is like a daily movement toward ultimate doom; the only remedy is a changed heart committed to following Jesus. The life in Christ is moves daily toward eternal life.

The Bible tells us that the wisdom of the world is foolishness in God's sight (1 Corinthians 3:19). The enemy uses the world's wisdom as a very effective weapon as it usually comes as quite a subtle attack. Christians need to recognize this subtle influence and protect themselves against it by putting on the full armor of God. Real wisdom comes from the fear of the Lord.

Wisdom acquired by following God's design for life enables us to avoid moral pitfalls and equips us with the skills to live a godly life. The wisdom of the Lord makes us wise sons of our heavenly Father. The Bible calls us craftsmen skilful in their trade (Exodus 31:3). The Book of Proverbs urges us to get wisdom: "Get wisdom, get understanding; do not forget my words or swerve from them" (Proverbs 4:5). The reason for this advice is because the wisdom that comes from God is worth more than silver or gold (Proverbs 3:13-14).

Jesus is our wisdom sent directly from God to mankind. Seek wisdom daily and you will increase in it and receive the ability for decision-making from above (Proverbs 2:10-11). Like Joseph and Daniel, the ability to make godly decisions will put us in high places with kings and provide us with riches and honor.

What Does This Fear of the Lord Mean to Us Personally?

The fear of the Lord springs from the recognition that our eternal God gave His beloved Son for us, taking upon himself our sin and misery. He gave His Son, our Lord Jesus Christ, to atone for our sins, and through our faith in Him we are saved and became joint heirs to the throne. This fear of the Lord emanates from the discovery that we did not merit this gift of sonship, but that it has nevertheless been given to us by grace through the love of a wonderful Father. When we discover that fear of the Lord is a prerequisite to a true relationship with the Father, we have embraced wisdom. When we embrace wisdom we discover that it is high time to awaken from sleep, to arise and live as the person we were really made to be, as members of God's elect—a chosen people. This revelation enables us to recognize that we are joint heirs to the throne with Christ, who set us free from our sin and misery.

The fear of the Lord should be very real to us individually. It should not be triggered by anxiety or intimidation, nor should the endless keeping of rules for it be inspired from our spirits and born of gratitude to Him. Fear of God is liberating and not restrictive, because it gives confidence about the true order of the world. When we fear Him, we will choose to live by His commands, which bring true freedom. Scripture tells us, "Good understanding have all those who do His commandments" (Psalm 111:10, NASV).

My question to all the readers is: Do you obey His commandments?

To fear the Lord and keep His commandments is to perform our duty as sons of the living God. The controlling factor of all life should be the fear of God, which means submission to God and to His revelation (Proverbs 1:7). Doesn't the certainty of God's unconditional and sacrificial love for us demand a response?

The Prophet Micah gave us an insight into understanding the qualities that are important to God. They are:

1. just behavior,
2. constant commitment to love, and
3. humble fellowship with Him (Micah 6:8)

To do this is an indication that you fear God and obey His commands.

SUMMARY

To summarize the above teaching—fear God and keep His commandments, for there is great benefit in doing so.

The Blessings of Holy Fear

• Like Jesus, we have assurance that our prayers will be answered by the Father. When we have holy fear, our hearts are positioned to receive answers from God (Hebrews 5:7).

• Like David, when we deposit our lives in the hands of God, we become partakers of the covenant blessing that He has stored up for His faithful servants (Psalm 31:19).

• Those who trust and obey the Lord will always shun evil and do good, and as a result they will lack no good thing (Psalm 34:8-14). According to Psalm 34, those who fear the Lord receive the following blessings: They are saved from trouble (verses 7, 17, and 22); they are happy (verse 8); their needs are met (verse 9); they receive good things from the Lord (verse 10); God listens to their prayers (verse 15); they receive solutions to their problems (verse 19); and they receive forgiveness for their sin (verse 22). What a glorious blessing!

• Those who fear the Lord and do His will receive superior wisdom and understanding from above (Proverbs 1:1-7 and 9:10-11).

• They will receive favor from men and things they had not asked for—houses full of all good things, which they did not fill (Deuteronomy 6:10-11).

- They will be under the protection of the Lord. No disaster, plague, or diseases will befall them, and He will drive away their fears (Psalm 91 and Psalm 115:11).
- Those who fear the Lord receive the peace that passes man's understanding (Philippians 4:7). and avoid the judgment that comes from ill-gotten treasures (Proverbs 10:2 and 15:16; Acts 9:31).
- They will receive divine guidance, clarity, and revelation and will enjoy the prosperity that comes from the Lord (Psalm 25:9-14).
- Like Solomon, those who fear the Lord will receive wisdom to be good leaders of God's people and enjoy rewarding lives.

Additional Benefits of Holy Fear

- Holy fear leads to life, contentment, and deliverance from every trouble that comes. The Bible puts it this way: "Many are the afflictions of the righteous, but the LORD delivers him from out of them all" (Psalm 34:19, NKJV).
- It provides answers to our deepest needs and produces a secure household (Exodus 1:21).
- It produces trustworthy and successful leaders who discharge their duties with integrity and honesty (Exodus 18:21).
- It results in enjoyment of our labor, favor, and blessings from the Lord and a rewarding life (Psalm 128:1-4).
- The Lord's compassion is upon those who fear Him (Psalm 103:13).
- His love is with those who fear Him, and His righteousness with their children's children (Psalm 103:17).

God's love and truth will always protect us; and His standards, as measured by the Word, will guide us into all truth. It is my prayer and desire that we will receive the faith to stand for truth and not lean on our own understanding. We need to remember that God's standard should be our standard.

I would like to leave you with Prophet Samuel's farewell speech after confirming Saul as king in 1 Samuel 12:23-25: "But I will teach you the good and the right way: Only fear the LORD, and serve him in truth with all your heart; for consider how great things he hath done for you. But if ye shall still do wickedly, ye shall be consumed, both ye and your king" (1 Samuel 12:23-25, KJV).

This prophecy was fulfilled in 1 Samuel 13:13-15 when Samuel rebuked Saul for not keeping the command of the Lord. The kingship was spiritually taken away from Saul, although he remained the natural king for a long time—in fact, for forty years (Acts 13:21). Brothers and Sisters in Christ, any time that you want to add to, delete, or refine God's commands, please remember Prophet Samuel's reply to Saul's defence: "Does the LORD delight in burnt offerings and sacrifices as much as in obeying the voice of the LORD? To obey is better than sacrifice, and to heed is better than the fat of rams" (1 Samuel 15:22).

Bible Verses to Help Us

1. "A son honoureth his father, and a servant his master: if then I be a father, where is mine honour? and if I be a master, where is my fear" (Malachi 1:6, KJV)? (Are you a son? If so, where is the fear of the Lord in your heart? Where is the respect that is due to the Lord?)
2. "The fear of the LORD is the beginning of wisdom, and the knowledge of the Holy One is understanding" (Proverbs 9:10).
3. "The fear of the LORD is the beginning of wisdom; a good understanding have all those who do His commandments; His praise endures forever" (Psalm 111:10, NASV).
4. "The angel of the LORD encamps around those who fear him, and he delivers them" (Psalm 34:7).
5. "But seek first the kingdom of God and His righteousness, and all these things shall be added to you" (Matthew 6:33, NKJV).
6. "Get wisdom, get understanding; do not forget my words or swerve from them" (Proverbs 4:5).
7. "If anyone acknowledges that Jesus is the Son of God, God lives in him and he in God" (1 John 4:15).
8. "The grass withers and the flowers fall, but the word of our God stands forever" (Isaiah 40:8).
9. "I am the way and the truth and the life. No one comes to the Father except through me" (John 14:6).
10. "I am the gate; whoever enters through me will be saved. He will come in and go out, and find pasture. The thief comes only to steal

and kill and destroy; I have come that they may have life, and have it to the full" (John 10:9).

11. "For even if there are so-called gods whether in heaven or on earth, as indeed there are many gods and many lords, yet for us there is but one God, the Father, from whom are all things, and we exist for Him; and one Lord, Jesus Christ, by whom are all things, and we exist through Him. However not all men have this knowledge" (1 Corinthians 8:5-7, NASV).

12. "'To whom will you compare me? Or who is my equal?' says the Holy One" (Isaiah 40:25).

13. "As for me, far be it from me that I should sin against the LORD by failing to pray for you. And I will teach you the way that is good and right. But be sure to fear the LORD and serve him faithfully with all your heart; consider what great things he has done for you. Yet if you persist in doing evil, both you and your king will be swept away" (1 Samuel 12:23-25).

14. "Then the church throughout Judea, Galilee and Samaria enjoyed a time of peace. It was strengthened; and encouraged by the Holy Spirit, it grew in numbers, living in the fear of the Lord" (Acts 9:31).

15. "Live as free men, but do not use your freedom as a cover-up for evil; live as servants of God. Show proper respect to everyone: Love the brotherhood of believers, fear God, honour the king" (1 Peter 2:16-17).

16. "From the west, men will fear the name of the LORD, and from the rising of the sun, they will revere his glory" (Isaiah 59:19).

17. "Who, then, is the man that fears the LORD? He will instruct him in the way chosen for him. He will spend his days in prosperity, and his descendants will inherit the land. The LORD confides in those who fear him; he makes his covenant known to them" (Psalm 25:12-14).

18. "But from everlasting to everlasting the Lord's is with those who fear him, and his righteousness with their children's children—with those who keep his covenant and remember to obey his precepts" (Psalm 103:17-18).

19. "As a father has compassion on his children, so the LORD has compassion on those who fear him" (Psalm 103:13).

20. "Unless the Lord builds the house, its builders labor in vain. Unless the LORD watches over the city, the watchmen stand guard in vain" (Psalm 127:1).
21. "And whatsoever we ask, we receive of him, because we keep his commandments, and do those things that are pleasing in his sight" (1 John 3:22, KJV).
22. "How great is your goodness, which you have stored up for those who fear you, which you bestow in the sight of men on those who take refuge in you" (Psalm 31:19).
23. "Praise the LORD. Blessed is the man who fears the LORD, who finds great delight in his commands. His children will be mighty in the land; the generation of the upright will be blessed. Wealth and riches are in his house, and his righteousness endures forever" (Psalm 112:1-3).

END NOTES

1. *Longman Modern English Dictionary* Longman, 1966.
2. *The Promise Bible* (Page 485 of the New Living Translation). Tyndale House Publishers, Inc.

TEN

THE VERDICT

Fear is a universal problem, as it transcends geographical region, age, gender, and social importance. It is not just a problem attributed to infancy, for it affects the weak, strong, old, and those who have seen and heard it all! Most of us suffer from all kinds of fears and insecurities at some point in our lives. Some of our fears are real, some unfounded; but they can torment us day and night. They sap our energy, weaken our hearts, and rob us of our God-given peace. They hinder our work, our progress, and gradually erode our relationships with friends, families, colleagues, our spouses, children, and ultimately with God.

In John 10:10 Jesus says, "The thief comes only to steal and kill and destroy; I have come that they may have life, and have it to the full."

Fear steals our joy and kills our confidence in going after the promises of our Lord Jesus. It keeps us from greatness and from being the best that God has created us to be. It also keeps us from living in the position of victory Jesus won for us.

Our main solution to the fear factor is rooted in the finished work of Christ. He is the only one who can set us free from the devastating effects of unhealthy fear. David declares in Psalm 27, "The LORD is my light and my salvation—whom shall I fear? The LORD is the stronghold of my life—of whom shall I be afraid?" (Psalm 27:1-3). The psalmist knew that God was the source of his strength and the only one to fear.

Psalm 46 assures us that believers need not be fearful, irrespective of war and natural disasters occurring around us; even if creation was to become uncreated our God would still be in control, His mighty power and sustaining presence sufficient for us.

In Matthew 28:20, Jesus assures us, "I am with you always, to the very end of the age" (Matthew 28:20).

If the Commander-in-Chief of the Heavenly armies is with us, who can be against us? The one with all the authority in Heaven and earth has promised to be with us always, even to the end of the world. Go on: serve your fears an eviction notice. Look your fears full in the face and declare, "The Lord is with me, and I shall fear no one or no thing." Then send an e-mail or *snail mail* to any of your friends who have been living with mixed emotions for a long time, saying, *"Do not be afraid, for the Lord is with you!"*

You will notice that we have explored, among other things, different levels of fear and the definition of fear and its causes. We have also conducted more detailed expositions on the fear of failure, fear of the Lord, fear of death, fear of change, and fear of man and have explored the relationship between fear and love. This verdict is a summary and conclusion of all our discussions with a specific focus on how to overcome these fears. Now that you have located the areas of fear in your life and in the lives of your loved ones, it is time to summarize how to overcome them. Like Satan, fear is your enemy and you need to apply the weapons of the Spirit to overcome it.

Below is a short summary of some of the fears mentioned in this book and how to overcome them through the practical application of the Word of God. A combination of one or more of the suggested methods may be employed to overcome your fear, irrespective of its causes.

Fear of the Unknown / Fear of Knowing God

The very thing we fear is usually the solution to our problem. Knowledge and experience of the thing we fear could be the perfect solution. If we are exposed to the things we fear in a non-threatening and controlled manner, we receive a gradual but certain deliverance from such things. For example, a fear of heights and a fear of water can be solved by supervised exposure to the focus of fear.

If you suffer from the fear of knowing God because of your strange misconception of Him, I implore you to let go of your hindrance and allow the Spirit of God to take control. When you do that, the first thing you will notice is His presence and revelation to you as a Father. You will begin to recognize that the Maker of Heaven and earth cannot be controlled or manipulated; instead He always upgrades your life as you submit to His authority and lordship. If your fear of knowing God is rooted in your failure to obey His commands or to live up to the standards set in the Bible, remember it was while we were still sinners that He sent His only son to die for us. If you are worrying that God will not accept you or has abandoned you, I can assure you that God does not forsake those who seek Him (Psalm 9:10).

THE HEALTHY FEAR OF DANGER

It is often said that a newborn baby has only two basic fears—the fear of falling and the fear of sudden loud noises. This is where, for the child, there are real possibilities of danger or harm. For example, attempting to cross the motorway or freeway presents a real danger of death by car accident. In addition, touching a live electric wire presents a real danger of electrocution and possibly death. When you fall behind with your mortgage payments, there is a real danger of repossession or loss of your home. All of the above can be overcome by having respect for the source of danger, by not exposing ourselves to dangerous environments, and by being good stewards of our finances. We need to recognize and act on our God-given, built-in fear indicators, which instinctively tell us, *"There is danger here! Please avoid it!"*

By listening to our inner voice, we don't need to laugh in the face of fear at all times, but sometimes just need to walk away from potentially dangerous situations when God triggers our in-built alarm systems. This self-preserving fear is good and profitable to mankind as it causes us to take responsibility for ourselves and others.

Unhealthy fear is the negative type of fear that imprisons its victims, taunts us with ridiculous phobias, controls by manipulation, and erodes all confidence and security. It kills every iota of love inside us and cuts all lines of communication with others. It may be caused by particular experiences or passed on to us by parents, relatives, teachers, and other people who have influenced our early years. Unhealthy fears are usually triggered by the enemy of our souls (the devil), whose only assignment is to destroy our peace. But Jesus has come to give us abundant life and freedom from all enslavement to fear.

THE FEAR OF MAN

Fear can come from human intimidation, fueled by irrational anxiety. This is when we are paralyzed by the thought of what man will do to us because of our failure or refusal to do certain things. Man may abuse us emotionally, by which I refer to someone with authority exercising power negatively over us, causing untold suffering and paralysis of our normal faculties to the extent that we live in constant fear. We need to realize that every human being should be respected but that only God should be feared. To trust and revere God ensures our safety, and gives us the wisdom to deal with all other false evidence that appears as real in our lives, while the fear of man is very dangerous (Proverbs 29:25).

If your ways are pleasing to God and you are doing His will, I can assure you that your angry enemies will lie down confused and ashamed because the Lord is your ever-present helper. Your sorrow and mourning will disappear, and you will be overcome with joy and gladness (Isaiah 35:10).

Instead of fearing man, you will be able to face him with courage and confidence because you know his limitations and that all men ultimately answer to God (Psalm 27:1-3).

Like King David, let your security be rooted in the Lord in the face of all that your enemies can do. Meditate on God's promises in Psalm 27, and you will be filled with the courage that comes from trusting in the presence of God.

And if your enemies prove to be worthy opponents, resisting the counsel of God, you need to be assured that, while the strongman may harm your body, he cannot touch your soul.

It is only God who can destroy both soul and body in hell, so fear Him alone (Matthew 10:28). Jesus looked Pontius Pilate in the face and was not afraid because He knew that man's power over Him was limited to that given by His Father in Heaven because He is the ultimate source of all power (John 19:8-11).

Jesus also stood His ground among the Sanhedrin, boldly facing His enemies and courageously speaking the truth, even though He was aware of the plot to kill Him (Matthew 26:57-68).

If you are overly timid, easily cowed, and afraid to speak up, ask God for help because He has not given us a spirit of timidity or fear, but one of love, boldness, and of a sound mind (2 Timothy 1:7).

If people-pleasing is your problem because you are afraid of what man can do to you, I urge you to reclaim your voice and cease to be a people pleaser. Purpose in your heart to become a God pleaser and to do His divine will.

By the inspiration of God, at the very center of the Bible is Psalm 118:8. I believe this is also the center of God's will because it says, "It is better to trust in the Lord than to put confidence in man" (NKJV).

Man will fail you, but God's Word can be trusted; it is not fickle and unreliable but is life-giving and eternal. It never fails but will surely come to pass.

His Word is forever settled in Heaven and therefore on earth. Second Corinthians 1:20 says, "For no matter how many promises God has made, they are 'Yes' in Christ. And so through him the 'Amen' is spoken by us to the glory of God" (2 Corinthians 1:20).

Jesus taught His disciples never to be afraid of those who can kill the body and after that can do no more, but to fear the one who after killing the body, has the power to throw us into hell (Luke 12:4-5). If you fear man instead of God, you will be ensnared because Proverbs 29:25-26 tells us, "Fear of man will prove to be a snare, but whoever trusts in the LORD is kept safe. Many seek an audience with a ruler, but it is from the LORD that man gets justice."

This tells us that the fear of man may lure us into trouble by shifting our trust from God to man, so that we forget, for example, that it is only God who gives us promotion and not the head of our company or department.

Finally, be assured that nothing can separate you from the love of God. If God is for you, who can be against you (Romans 8:31-39)? Remember that you have been sentenced to a life of victory in Christ

Jesus because of His love for you and His finished work on the Cross of Calvary.

THE FEAR OF FAILURE

As mentioned earlier, Satan uses failures to get you to listen to him. The degree of relentless attack on you should give you an idea of the wonderful plan God has for your life. Like the servant with one talent, the fear of failure can prevent you from taking hold of what God has already given to you. Such fear can keep you from testing your God-given skill in the marketplace and prevent you from profiting from using the wisdom and good judgment that comes from the Lord.

You need to recognize and learn the lessons taught through failure and be positive that all things work together for the good of those who love the Lord (Romans 8:28). Remember that your failure will only be an opportunity for God to reveal His great success as His power is mighty in our weaknesses.

Peter was a human being just like you and me. He had to face his fears when he stepped out and walked on the water to meet Jesus. Peter lost his focus on Jesus temporarily because when he saw the boisterous waves he was afraid and began to sink. But the storm and the angry sea did not stop Peter from stepping out into a breakthrough. Like Peter, we need to cry out to Jesus for help. He is waiting to take our hands so that we may victoriously walk on the road to success again (Matthew 14:31).

David encouraged himself in the Lord after suffering the loss of his family and his whole community. We need to employ David's coping strategy because it is a winning formula. Scripture tells us that after hearing a word from the Lord, David pursued the invaders and returned home with all the captives and a great bounty (1 Samuel 30:4-20). This is our portion in Jesus' name. The end of the matter will be better than the beginning (Ecclesiastes 7:8). Give your failures to the Lord and watch Him turn them into an uncommon blessing.

The enemy may have infiltrated your mind with negative thoughts to the extent that you have grown to expect the worst outcome regarding the important people in your life. Please stop listening to the voice of the enemy, tune in your antenna to the Lord, and focus on

God's Word, which promises success. There was a very successful and prosperous businessman in New York who created his own private mental pictures in which his company was forced into bankruptcy. The more he ran this mental picture of failure, the more he sank into deep depression. He eventually went bankrupt. All the things he feared came to pass. These things did not initially exist, but he brought them to pass by constantly fearing, believing, and expecting financial disaster. The pious Job suffered the same fate as our businessman above. He exclaimed, "What I feared has come upon me; what I dreaded has happened to me" (Job 3:25).

In order to overcome the fear of failure, we must take responsibility for our failure and resist the temptation to blame someone or the system. We must start confessing positively, remove impossibility, and replace it with possibility such as, "With man this is impossible, but not with God; all things are possible with God" (Mark 10:27). Or "I can do everything through him who gives me strength" (Philippians 4:13).

Seek good counsel because there is wisdom in a multitude of counselors (Proverbs 24:6). We need to put failures behind us and strive forward to reach new goals ahead. A confident attitude and a good prayer life will help us start again with a clean sheet, and we will yet praise the Lord for new visions and their successful implementation. A determined heart will take us closer to our dream. By this, I do not mean that we exchange the spirit of fear for one of stubbornness. But to purpose in our hearts that success is our portion, because in this frame of mind we are focused and determined to succeed irrespective of circumstances or limitations.

Success is a state of mind. We feel success, we see success, we think success, we work toward success, and refine our success strategies by sharpening, modifying, and upgrading our modes of operation. Remember that it is the Lord who gives power to make wealth. We must acknowledge Him and take our plans to Him by seeking His counsel. His plan must be our plan because we recognize that unless the Lord builds the house, its builders labor in vain (Psalm 127:1).

Remember that Scripture says, "For a just man falleth seven times, and riseth up again: but the wicked shall fall into mischief" (Proverbs 24:16, KJV).

If your failures are the result of the enemy's plan to ruin you because you are a righteous person, be assured that by the blessing and wisdom of God upon your life you will rise up again. In the event that temptation has taken you by surprise and you have fallen seven times into sin, leading to your eventual fall from grace, I have come to encourage you to repent and allow the grace and mercy of God to be made available to you so that the peace that passes human understanding can descend upon you (Philippians 4:7). When you achieve that, the wicked person who expected to see your ruin will fail and fall into mischief and utter destruction.

Finally, be fully persuaded that God's plan is to prosper you and not to harm you; He plans to give you hope and a future (Jeremiah 29:11). Give your past failures to God and trust Him to rise above those situations for you because you know He is fully in control of the past and certainly in control of your future. His marvelous grace covers all your failures, so tell those gloating wicked people, "Do not rejoice over me, my enemy; when I fall, I will arise; when I sit in darkness, the LORD will be a light to me" (Micah 7:8, NKJV).

I also encourage you to personalize this declaration and confess it daily: "I will trust in the Lord with all of my heart, and I will not lean on my own understanding. In all my ways I will acknowledge Him, and He will surely make my paths straight" (Proverbs 3:5-6).

The Fear of Death

We need to recognize that death is the result of the fallen state of mankind and probably the cause of more secret concern than most of us care to admit. Death has become a taboo subject even among counselors, pastors, and ministers. But we need to be aware that repressing frank discussion about this subject is unhealthy. Life and death belong to God. Everything else has been put under our control (Genesis 1:26-28). In other words, do not fear something that is beyond your control.

Jesus suffered death, so that by the grace of God He might taste death for everyone (Hebrews 2:9); His resurrection is a clear signal of our resurrection. Jesus transformed death into new life, which shows us Christians that we should not fear death because the power that resurrected Jesus is still available to us today.

John 3:16 promises us that through the eyes of love God gave His beloved Son, that whoever believes in Him shall not perish but have eternal life. All those who have died in Christ are only asleep; they will all rise again (1 Thessalonians 4:14). But those who are not in Christ Jesus need to be afraid of death because they will only rise to shame and everlasting contempt (Daniel 12:2).

There is a real loss in death. We must not deny this, for to do so is to create a delusion. It is the way we think about the loss that is most important. If we adopt a negative approach, a loss could send us to the edge of depression, to the extent that we find no reason to continue living. A positive approach involves accepting the loss, confronting it by grieving, and then moving on. The Lord accepted the loss of intimate fellowship with Adam and Eve; then He gave us the second Adam (Jesus) to put things right and save us from self-destruction. In Jesus we gain access back to the Father, but we have to believe in Him to save our soul. Our challenge is not to respond with fear, but to embrace the loss and allow it to give us a sense of urgency in fulfilling God's plan for our lives.

When we let fear guide our decisions, we remain stuck and become paralyzed. Jesus became flesh, fought and won victory over death, and by virtue of His finished work delivered those who have lived their lives as slaves to the fear of dying (Hebrews 2:14-15).

The Church must give hope to the hopeless and call humanity to a right relationship with God, our Creator, who loves humanity so much that He willingly gave His only Son for us as a sacrifice for our sin. We should not allow the seeds of denial and unbelief in the finished work of Christ to germinate in people's minds because such seeds do not give hope or purpose to the children of God. As we recognize and affirm what Jesus did for humanity 2,000 years ago, we become unafraid of death because we are convinced beyond reasonable doubt that Christ has won the victory over death (Hebrews 2:14-15).

Christians should remember and affirm the saying of Jesus, "I am the resurrection, and the life: he that believeth in me, though he were dead, yet shall he live" (John 11:25, KJV). Children of the living God, do not fear death because physical death is not the end of life. Instead it is the door to eternal life for those who believe in Jesus Christ.

Believers, let us share this message with as many as we come across, so that we may depopulate hell, and populate Heaven, thereby removing the fear of death from people's minds because Jesus has already won victory over death. For as many as put their faith in Him shall be saved and rescued from the sting of physical death because they will live eternally with the Father.

Life after death is real. When Christ comes again, those who belong to Him will be raised to life, and then the end will come. At that time Christ will destroy all rulers, authorities, and powers, and He will hand over the kingdom to God the Father. Christ must rule until He puts all enemies under His control. The last enemy to be destroyed will be death (1 Corinthians 15:23-26).

Guilt Leads to Fear

Guilt can lead to fear when we fear the repercussions of our wrongdoing. We could call it the fear of punishment. The main remedies for this are the confession of sin and the avoidance of blame-shifting and excuses. That was the solution to the Prodigal Son's problem. He confessed his sin, repented, and was restored by the Father, who is always rejoicing with the host of Heaven when sinners receive a new heart by surrendering to the lordship of Jesus.

Adam and Eve, when they disobeyed God, felt guilty and fled out of fear, covering themselves in an attempt to hide from God. They could have confessed their sin, which would have led to forgiveness instead of their being cast out of the Garden of Eden. In dealing with the first couple, God confronted them, but instead of dealing with them as He dealt with Satan's rebellion, He gave them hope and tempered His judgement with mercy. Instead of eternal separation like Satan, they got the promise of a Messiah who would reconcile man to God (Genesis 3:15) by destroying the work of the deceiver and tempter.

Nathan confronted David. Christ also confronted Peter, after his denial. In like manner, everyone suffering from fear through wrongdoing should be confronted directly and restored after undergoing the due counseling process. However, we must be mindful of people's feelings and state of mind. We should show a genuine concern for the person as a whole, allowing for the Lord's conviction. We should not focus on condemnation. When this method is used appropriately, it facilitates rapport and confidence between counselor and counselee, with the result that confession may come easy. Forgiveness in Christ will then lead to restoration.

At times the above method does not work with some people. In these cases we need to pull out the truth by force in order to provide quality help. This is a process Jay Adams refers to as "Yanking."[1] Remember that Christ restructured Peter's life when he was in utter despair, for his life had been shattered over his denial (John 21:15-19). However, Peter was restored, and a radical change took place in his life. He became the *Rock*. So will you and those you counsel in Jesus' name.

THE FEAR OF THE LORD

According to Ecclesiastes 12:13, we need to fear God and keep His commandments as this is the whole duty of man. God has commanded us to live joyfully, responsibly, and wisely. The controlling factor of all of life should be the fear of God, which is the submission to God and to His revelation (Proverbs 1:7).

When we are afraid of death, failure, and changes, we have anxiety, which is different from the fear of the Lord. Anxiety has nothing to do with the fear of the Lord. Equally, fear of the Lord is different to fearing God because we think He is great, mighty, and ready to punish our mistakes or might possibly condemn us to everlasting hell. This is a false fear of the Lord, and the best name for it is anxiety. The remedy for anxiety is to locate the source and circumstances that fill you with this condition and apply the Word of God to it. One such word is, "Be careful for nothing; but in every thing by prayer and supplication with thanksgiving let your requests be made known unto God. And the peace of God, which passeth all understanding, shall keep your hearts and minds through Christ Jesus" (Philippians 4:6-7, KJV).

As we change from anxiety to a healthy fear of the Lord, we discover that God has loved and chosen us, has made a covenant with us, and has promised to be with us always. We come into a sudden realization that we have been set free from our sin and eternal condemnation. So what could we possibly have to fear?

The fear of the Lord is the beginning of wisdom. It is more than knowledge, more than understanding; it is more than the collation of facts and theology but is the kind of insight and foreknowledge that the world cannot give us. As we enter into Christ's finished work on the Cross, we begin to live beyond death; we begin to live eternally on this earth. It takes divine wisdom for us to recognize the wonderful life Jesus has given to us through His shed blood on the Cross.

If we are looking for riches and power, the best place to find them is from the Lord. Psalm 24:1 puts it like this, "The earth is the LORD'S, and the fulness thereof; the world, and they that dwell therein" (Psalm 24:1, KJV).

This tells us that all we ever wanted—peace, joy, power, healing, powerful contacts, property, and wealth—all belong to the Lord. And when we align ourselves with the King of all kings and obey all His commands, we are strategically positioned to receive our heart's desires according to His will.

Solomon recognized his frailties and requested wisdom, and God granted him wisdom, riches, honor, and the anointing to function in his role. Solomon was not short-changed by anyone; instead, he received things he had not asked for, houses full of every good thing, which he did not fill (Deuteronomy 6:10-11).

When you choose to put all your faith in God, you will realize that the jar of flour will not be used up and the jug of oil will not run dry until the Lord gives rain on the land (1 Kings 17:14).

My theology is simple: Be aligned with the owner of Heaven and earth rather than pursuing the created things.

When you have Jesus, you become joint heir to the throne and inherit everything by virtue of being a blood relation. Let praise come from your heart because God inhabits the praises of His people (Psalm 22:3).

A heart full of praise cannot be a fearful one, because praise and worship bring us into the presence of our awesome God.

Remember that Jesus gave us authority over all the power of the enemy, and it is our duty to use it effectively in interceding in order to counter the spirit of fear in our lives and in the lives of our brethren. When Jehoshaphat was afraid of "the Moabites and Ammonites with some of the Meunites" (2 Chronicles 20:1-30), he decided to pray to God, and he overcame by the mighty power of prayer. You have the weapon—use it!

Trusting in God is the ultimate remedy for fear. The more consumed with fear we become, the more distant God seems to be. Our ultimate victory over fear depends on our walk with the Lord. Seek Him daily; develop intimacy with Him through prayer and reading His Word, the Bible. As you draw near to God, the Holy Spirit will fill and empower you daily, and the spirit of fear will disappear from your life.

We cannot know God's strength until we know His Son. If you have never acknowledged Jesus as your Savior, now is the best time to do so. Simply pray and ask Jesus to come into your heart to be your Savior and Lord. To help you pray this prayer effectively, a template prayer has been designed for you in Appendix 1—"The Decision"— located at the back of this book.

THE FEAR OF CHANGE

The world is changing, people are changing, and the conditions in which we live today are rapidly changing. The way we evangelize today is changing fast; even the devil is changing the way he operates. Change is taking place every day, whether we acknowledge its occurrence or not. While Europe is regressing in its passion to reach the lost world, other continents are being empowered to take the gospel of our Lord Jesus Christ to those areas that have previously been denied the Word of God.

In the midst of these changes, some people are still holding out for constancy or finding it difficult to make lasting changes in their lives. Jesus has always been interested in our inward changes and our spiritual transformation from the kingdom of darkness to the Kingdom of light. It should be comforting to know that God meets us in the midst of these changes. Times of change should give us special opportunities to catch a glimpse of God in an unprecedented way and to grow in intimacy with Him. Abram was called to intimacy with

God. Although in the process he lied and trusted in his own strength, he later received a change of name (Abraham) and a change of fortune (father of nations).

We need the help and presence of God to win victory against a multitude of credible oppositions and circumstances that seek to frustrate our journey with change. The first step to conquering the fear of change is to call on God for strength to confront it, rather than seeking temporary relief through avoidance tactics. When God was about to relocate the Israelites and change their future by taking them to the promised land, they suddenly became afraid at the sight of the Egyptian army. Moses assured them of God's sovereign control over all things. He told the people, "Do not be afraid. Stand firm and you will see the deliverance the LORD will bring you today. The Egyptians you see today you will never see again. The LORD will fight for you; you need only to be still" (Exodus 14:13-14).

Believers, the Lord who brought the Israelites from a place of slavery to the land of freedom is still on the throne and is not only able but also willing to bring you out of the stronghold of slavish fear. Your part of the bargain is to place your trust in Him and then watch things unfold. Psalm 37:4-6 says, "Delight yourself in the LORD and he will give you the desires of your heart. Commit your way to the LORD; trust in him and he will do this: He will make your righteousness shine like the dawn, the justice of your cause like the noonday sun."

People will make promises one day but disappoint you the next. God's faithfulness and love, however, are not subject to the fluctuations of time, space, or human mortality. He does not suffer from fickle whims, irrational mood swings, or the inability to handle circumstances. His Word never changes and never fails.

Let your fearful situation be changed through prayer and your knowledge of God's Word. Avoid complaining and choose to be changed. Be determined to be dead to the old sinful nature and to let Christ live through you. Then you can declare, "I have been crucified with Christ and I no longer live, but Christ lives in me. The life I live in the body, I live by faith in the Son of God, who loved me and gave himself for me" (Galatians 2:20).

The above passage is a declaration of positive change. We also see Paul's willingness to change by leaving the old lifestyle in order to enjoy the inheritance of a son. True change is never effortless; you must be committed to the process for change to occur. You, too, can change as you allow Jesus to bring the necessary changes into your life and as you invest time, money, and effort toward a particular focus. The most important change agents are prayer and a commitment to fellowship with God in worship and obedience to His Word.

From Fear to Love

The Bible says, "There is no fear in love. But perfect love drives out fear, because fear has to do with punishment. The one who fears is not made perfect in love" (1 John 4:18).

This tells us that godly love is the antidote to fear. When we fight each other, leading to stress, migraines, and loss of joy, it is because we are not walking in forgiveness; and pride has taken root in our hearts. Light and darkness cannot co-habit, so when pride and discord move into the very place where the Spirit of God lives, love disappears.

The spiritual prescription for living abundantly and flowing fully in the fruit of the Spirit is mentioned in Galatians 5:22—to specialize in love, joy, peace, patience, kindness, goodness, faithfulness, gentleness, and self-control. When we do this, fear evaporates and takes a permanent leave of absence. Jesus also encourages us to specialize in love (Mark 12:30). The Bible tells us that God is love. Our heavenly Father demonstrated His unconditional love for mankind by giving His only Son to be the ultimate sacrifice for our sin.

Love will position us for the indwelling and inflowing of the Holy Spirit because love is the nature of God. As we operate in God's nature, we have access to His supernatural power. We become human carriers of God's love to everyone who comes our way, bringing healing, deliverance from fear, and, ultimately, freedom. We need to know and be fully persuaded that God loves us because intellectual knowledge is not enough; it is the Holy Spirit who can give this assurance and enable us to walk in the most excellent way: the way of love.

David was fully persuaded of God's love. He declared in Psalm 23:4, "Even though I walk through the valley of the shadow of death,

I will fear no evil, for you are with me; your rod and your staff, they comfort me."

In Ephesians 3:16-20, Paul expresses a prayer that grows out of his awareness of all that God is doing in believers. He tells us in verses 16, 18, and 20 that God's key gifts are power and love. Such love can only be known through an intimate relationship with Jesus Christ.

In 1 John 4:18, John defines fear and love as being mutually exclusive. Love is from God, and whoever lives in love lives in God. Fear is from Satan, because it has to do with punishment or condemnation. Violence and aggression are unlikely to cast out fear but may actually be a trigger for further violence, escalating from fear. The good news is that we have the assurance of God's love, which erases all fear. It is logical that the best way to put off fear is to put on love by measuring our actions in accordance with the guidance given to us in 1 Corinthians 13:4-5.

If we are to walk in perfect love in order to cast out all fears, are there any further benefits of doing so? Below is a list of the possible benefits of walking in love. I like to call them The Ten L's of God's Love.

1. Love sets us free from unnecessary stress.
2. Love enhances the quality of our prayer life.
3. Love makes it possible for us to focus on the needs of others and give them due precedence.
4. Love for God gives us the ability to walk in accordance with His commandments.
5. Love gives us a good foundation so that we are like the house built on a rock.
6. Love and forgiveness ensures that nothing hinders our anointing.
7. Love enables us to grow in grace and absolute dependence on God.
8. Love helps our growth in the knowledge of the Lord and the free flow of His supernatural power.
9. Love empowers us to become an effective witness for God, as our relationship with Him enables us to talk about God in a loving and convincing manner.

10. Love for others and growth in the knowledge of the Lord equips us to become merciful like Jesus and provides the ability to forgive others.

By love, I refer to the highest and noblest form of love, which sees something infinitely precious in its object. This is the kind of love one has toward God, and it is the kind of love God has for us and is good in all circumstances. It is the kind of love that the Apostle John talks about in John 3:16, and the love that propels the Father to put all things into the Son's hands (John 3:35). I am talking about *agape* love.

If we must covet anything, let it be love because love never fails; it does not insist on its own right or its own way. It always seeks the best for other people. It is not arrogant but is sacrificial. Fear is no match for love: perfect love casts out fear.

The Last Word

Having concluded the reading of *The Fear Factor*, I pray that you will have already begun to find peace and freedom from fear through the truth of God's Word. It is my desire that your deliverance and freedom should be made permanent by putting God first in everything you do and remaining in a loving relationship with Jesus.

I pray that you are covered by God through the power of love that casts out all fears and that in your walk with Jesus you will become more and more like Him. Amen!

End Notes

1. "Yanking" is like forcing information out of people even in painful circumstances. The term was used by Jay E. Adams on page 174 of *Competent to Counsel*, Grand Rapids, Michigan: Zondervan Publishing House, 1970.

APPENDIXES

APPENDIX 1 — THE DECISION

SALVATION PRAYER TEMPLATE

"'In the time of my favor I heard you, and in the day of salvation I helped you.' I tell you, now is the time of God's favor, now is the day of salvation." (2 Corinthians 6:2)

Like the Prophet Jeremiah, if I say, "'I will not mention him or speak any more in his name,' his word is in my heart like a fire, a fire shut up in my bones. I am weary of holding it in; indeed, I cannot." (Jeremiah 20:9)

If you have been reading this book and have seen the various references to Appendix 1, the Salvation Prayer Template, and how to turn your life around and begin a wonderful relationship with Jesus, *now is the time.*

Jesus has made provisions for your sin. He paid the penalty for the sins of all mankind on the Cross. It does not matter what you have done in the past; whether you are a murderer, thief, drug dealer, prostitute, sorcerer, magician, freemason, Muslim, Buddhist, Hindu, or evil consultant, *everyone* is covered by His finished work on the Cross.

THE CALL

If you do not know Jesus or have not confessed Him as your personal Savior, *now* is the day of salvation. Do not let the enemy of your soul put fear inside you. Jesus says, "All that the Father gives me will come to me, and whoever comes to me I will never drive away" (John 6:37).

He has not changed. The assurance is still there for you today, as it was yesterday, especially for those who claim to be too intelligent or sophisticated for such *holy stuff*.

Are you saying, "I go to church and have answered a call like this sometime ago, yet nothing changes?" Make a renewed commitment to grow in the knowledge of Him. Walk with the Lord like never before.

Are you a Muslim, Freemason, Buddhist, Hindu, or from a different religion? Do you believe there are many ways to God? I tell you the strong veil of religion is still masking the truth from you. You can remove it today by changing to the camp of light. Jesus says to you, "No one can see the kingdom of God unless he is born again" (John 3:3).

Are you like Nicodemus (John 3:1-15), a religious leader who was caught up in the religious world? Are you living in a world of chronic darkness, ignorance, and misinformation, entrenched in the Law of Moses but not born from above by the renewal of the Spirit? You have never asked Jesus to come into your heart. God says that we are not saved by good works (Ephesians 2:8-9). Do not let pride keep you away.

Are you thinking that God is useless? Are you saying, "Where is God in my suffering? Is He watching to see when we do wrong things so He can punish us?" Let me assure you that God's eye has been on you ever since you were born. But not so that He can criticize you. God has a plan for you and wants to enjoy a relationship with you. He wants you to be happy and loves you so much that He willingly gave His one and only Son, so that everyone who believes in Him can have eternal life (John 3:16).

You do not have to be perfect for God to care about you. Everyone has messed things up at some time. No one can make himself or herself perfect by trying. And God is too great to be stopped by your failures or fears.

Simply pray the following prayer in faith and Jesus will be your Lord. The prison door will be opened so that you can walk through to Jesus. Let your life begin again today.

SALVATION PRAYER

Heavenly Father, I come to you in the name of Jesus.

Your Word says in Romans 10:9, "If you confess with your mouth, 'Jesus is Lord,' and believe in your heart that God raised him from the dead, you will be saved." And in Romans 10:13, your Word says, "Everyone who calls on the name of the Lord will be saved." In John 3:5-6 and Romans 8:9-11, you said my salvation would be the result of your Holy Spirit giving me new birth by coming to live in me. And in Luke 11:3 and Acts 2:4 you said you would fill me with your Spirit and give me the ability to speak with other tongues.

I take you at your Word. I confess that Jesus is Lord and turn away from a life of sin. And I believe in my heart that you raised Him from the dead. Thank you for coming into my heart, for giving me your Holy Spirit as you have promised, and for being Lord of my life. In Jesus' name, Amen!

If you have prayed this prayer, you have been "born again." That is, you have been made a new creature in Christ. Your past does not belong to you anymore. Your life has begun again. When Satan comes around trying to remind you of all your past deeds, just tell him, "Wrong door, you cannot come in. Sin no longer lives here!"

Having confessed Jesus as your Lord and Savior, you need to tell someone to witness to the fact that you now want to walk with God and find a Bible-believing church where you can have fellowship with believers. Make sure you also regularly read the Word of God as this gives truth and direction (Psalm 119:105). Irrespective of what circumstances life throws your way, He has promised that no one can take His children out of His hand (John 10:28). His presence surrounds you; the bond between you and the Lord cannot be broken.

NOTE: If you have received Jesus as your Lord and Savior using the above call to salvation, please share your story with us by sending an email message to akeem@thefearfactorbooks.com. We promise to continue praying for you so that you may enter fully into Jesus' finished work on the Cross. We pray that your new life will be permanent, in Jesus name, Amen.

APPENDIX 2
FEAR CHECKLIST NOTEBOOK
(Self-Help Section)

List your known fear and locate the Scripture or a combination of Scriptures that provides the perfect solution to it. Memorize and confess it daily from your spirit.

'WHAT DO YOU FEAR?' CHECKLIST

Your Fear	Causes of Fear	Time/ Circumstances[1]	Solution Rooted in God's Word

[1]Time/Circumstances. The purpose of this column is to assist you in determining a relationship between your fear and your environment, whether the fear was triggered at a particular time or due to a unique circumstance.

YOUR REFLECTIONS
After Keeping a Diary for Weeks/Months/Years

APPENDIX 3
PERSONAL DAILY CONFESSION & DECLARATION

Daily Confession

Father in Heaven, the Bible tells me in Second Timothy 1:7 that you have not given me a spirit of fear, but of power, love, and a sound mind. I confess that I have been operating contrary to your Word by living in fear and believing the lies of the enemy. I sincerely repent.

Thank you for opening the eyes of my mind so that I may discern every area of my life where I have been living contrary to your Word. From now on, I boldly apply the medicine of your Word to these areas (*Name those areas already identified in the Fear Checklist and any other areas that come to mind*) and I reject all the lies of the enemy.

Declaration

I recognize that the love of God casts out all fears, and I choose to deal with people around me in love as commanded by your Word.

I apply the weapon of love as part of my defensive armor against the spirit of fear because the Bible tells me that perfect love casts out all fear.

I desire to live a responsible, powerful, and fulfilling life with the help of your Holy Spirit. By faith, I overcome every fear in my life and gain victory over anxiety. I am now free in Christ Jesus by virtue of His finished work on the Cross. In Jesus' name, Amen.

ACKNOWLEDGMENTS

No one could write a book of such importance and clarity without assistance from others. I give all the glory to my Lord and Savior Jesus Christ, without whose sustaining presence only He knows where I would be. He is the one who gave birth to this book as a gift to the world at large. My highest appreciation for Your finished work on the Cross! I love You, Lord!

Without a shadow of doubt, the Holy Spirit is the main Author of this book; I am just in a privileged position as co-author. I thank my special Friend and Counselor, the Spirit of God, who has made my heart a place worthy of His presence. Holy Spirit, I love and appreciate You in my life!

Many thanks to Vera Agun, who through divine inspiration kept reminding me to write this book. Get ready for the harvest!

My gratitude to Pastor Michael Omawumi Efueye, the resident pastor of House on the Rock (the London Lighthouse Parish). I thank you for your editing, strategic guidance, and anointed teaching. It is a blessing to feed under an anointed teacher such as yourself. Pastor Omawunmi, you are not only a teacher of the Word; you practice it and have the heart of a shepherd. Stay blessed!

To Pastor Paul Adefarasin, the senior pastor and founding father of House on the Rock worldwide. I thank the Lord for making you a great visionary leader and for indirectly encouraging me to complete this book through your exhortation, validation, and preaching. The peculiar anointing you carry upon your life is now flowing from the shepherd to your sons in Christ, bringing healing to lives and deliverance to people under the bondage of fear.

My appreciation to Rodney Woods, resident pastor of City Temple Holborn Viaduct, London, who read, critiqued, edited, and encouraged me all the way. Your seed will surely germinate, and you shall reap a thousandfold.

It is always a blessing when you find a good wife who really complements you and makes up for your blind spots. Rufiat, I thank you for all your editing work, not only of this book but of all my many writings. Our heavenly Father will reward your labor of love.

The Amiaka brothers (Buzz, Chima, and Ikwu), Sharif Gbadamosi, Jumoke Fashakin, Ian Picken, Mrs. Sarah Rae, Steve and Stephanie Edmonds, Sandra (aka Rhianne Coles), Pastors Ayo and Dupe Gbajabiamila, Joseph Jesuthasann, and all other people not mentioned, I thank you all for contributing and co-editing this work. To all of you praying for me all over the world and to all my co-editors out there, I say, "Thank you!" God knows your names. May your needs be met by the only one who answers all prayer.

I would like to thank all the members of the defunct Adepta Christian Fellowship, the Alpha Course Management Team of the City Temple, and the Altar Care Team members of House on the Rock. All of you have believed in me, provided me with a platform to share the Word of God with you, served as a sounding board, or influenced me in ways beyond your imagination. God bless you all!

My gratitude in Christ to Steve Troxel of God's Daily Word Ministries, fellow authors and co-workers in God's kingdom, for directly and indirectly influencing my writings. I am deeply indebted to you all. Some of your names have been accredited in the endnotes. Geoff Shattock of Worknet, UK, you do not know me but your weekly series on fear has been a source of encouragement at the time of writing the manuscript for this book.

Finally, I would like to thank my chief editor Louise Gunn of Scribe Writing & Editorial Services, who transformed this book into a respectable and credible literary piece worthy of bringing glory to God.

Surely this book is a product of teamwork that has yielded much fruit. Thank you all for sowing the seed that has germinated to give life to others.